Safety Tips

real kids/real science books contain lots of ideas and suggestions for observing and collecting animals and plants in woods, fields, ponds, drainage ditches, and at the shore. If you follow a few simple rules, your adventures will be safe and enjoyable.

▶ Plan your field trips with your parents or guardian, even if you are going to collect or observe in a familiar place. Make sure they are aware if you need to venture into even shallow water.

▶ Wear appropriate dress. Protect your feet when wading; protect your arms and legs in heavy underbrush.

▶ Share your adventures with a friend.

real kids
real science
BOOKS

Meet the Arthropods...

"Study nature, not books." —LOUIS AGASSIZ

real kids
real science
BOOKS

Orthoptera

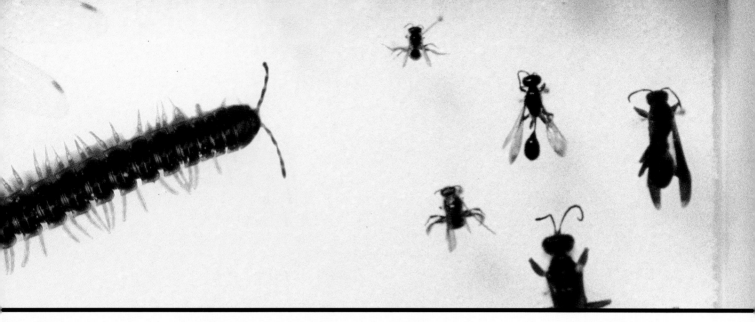

Meet the Arthropods...

written by Ellen Doris
original photography by Len Rubenstein

PRODUCED IN ASSOCIATION WITH
The Children's School of Science
Woods Hole, Massachusetts

T&H THAMES AND HUDSON

coleoptera

What is this book about?

Arthropods, animals with exoskeletons and jointed limbs, make up about three-quarters of all the animal species on Earth. This book focuses on members of six classes of arthropods, most of which should be quite easy for you to collect and observe. You will find lots of projects, field trips, ideas, and suggestions for exploring the world of arthropods.

How to use this book

Meet the Arthropods . . . is organized as a collection of separate experiments, investigations, and discoveries. It shows you where to look for arthropods and how to study them once you find them. Though some basic terms and concepts are introduced in the first few sections, you don't have to follow the book step-by-step from beginning to end. Look for a field trip that is easy to do near your home. Or you may want to go to your local supermarket to look at a lobster as described on page 30. Also, this book will be a lot more fun if you share some of the projects with someone else, a friend or a parent.

Where can you get specimens to study? And equipment?

First of all, try to collect specimens yourself. Many of them, such as spiders, flies, dragonflies, and beach crabs, are easy to find. Also, try to adapt what you have at home into equipment, including old buckets, dishpans, jars, and fish tanks. But you'll also find that you can order almost all the animals mentioned in this book, either live or preserved for observation, from biological supply houses at reasonable costs. There is a list of supply houses on page 62, but don't feel that you have to start ordering right away. You'll be surprised at how much you can find and make for yourself.

What is a cephalothorax? And how do I pronounce Merostomata?

Check out the Glossary on page 63, which defines all the terms that are printed in **bold** type. But don't get bogged down trying to pronounce long Latin names; sound them out as well as you can and go on.

Think for yourself

You'll probably have to adapt some of the projects you find in this book. You may not live near an ocean, a field, or a pond. But most big city parks have a wide range of insects, spiders, and aquatic arthropods. Remember, not every project works according to plan. Think about why things didn't go as planned, and try again.

The Children's School of Science
Woods Hole, Massachusetts

Each summer, in an old-fashioned schoolhouse whose rooms are crowded with plants, nets, microscopes, and bubbling aquaria, several hundred children between the ages of seven and sixteen attend classes for two hours each morning. Led by teachers who are experts in their field, the children take frequent field trips and work with each other on projects and experiments. The classes are informal, and courses range from Seashore Exploration to Ornithology to Neurobiology. For over seventy-five years, this remarkable institution has fostered the joy of discovery by encouraging direct observation of natural phenomena.

Contents

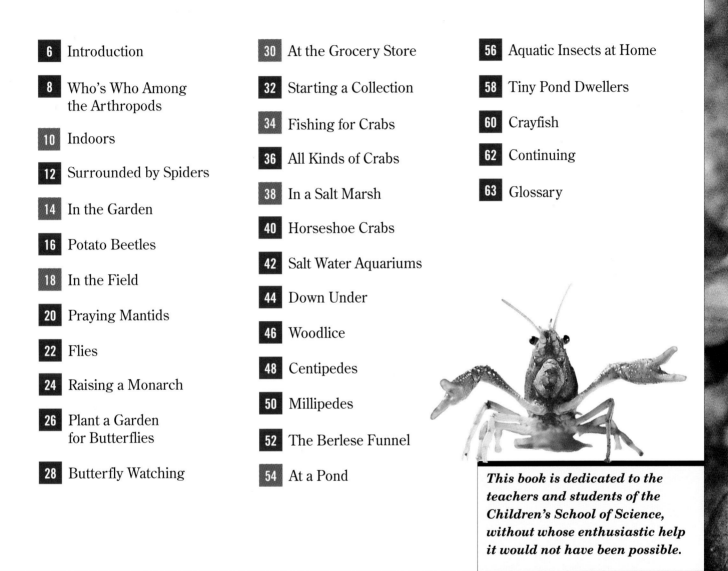

This book is dedicated to the teachers and students of the Children's School of Science, without whose enthusiastic help it would not have been possible.

Copyright © 1996 Thames and Hudson Inc., New York
First published in the United States in 1996 by Thames and Hudson Inc.,
500 Fifth Avenue, New York, New York 10110

Photos copyright © Len Rubenstein unless otherwise indicated.

Library of Congress Catalog Card Number 95-61699

Design, typesetting, and pre-press production by Beth Tondreau Design/Robin Bentz ■ Managing Editor, Laurance Rosenzweig

Color separations made by The Sarabande Press ■ Printed and bound in Hong Kong

Introduction

Even if you have never heard the word *arthropod* before, you are probably familiar with many animals that belong to this group. Spiders are arthropods, and so are crabs, beetles, crayfish, and centipedes. Arthropods live in the air, on the land, underground, and at the shore. This book will help you learn more about some of the common and interesting arthropods that live alongside you.

But what is an arthropod, anyway?

Scientists divide all of the animals that now live on Earth into about 26 large groups called **phyla**. Each phylum is a broad collection of animals with important things in common. Arthropods, the animals that make up the phylum Arthropoda, have a hard skin called an **exoskeleton** that covers their bodies. This exoskeleton supports and protects the structures inside the body. Arthropods also have jointed legs. In addition, many arthropods have bodies that are made up of small sections, or segments. Sometimes these seg-

This beetle is an arthropod. It has hard skin, jointed legs and body segments.

ments are easy to see, but other times they are hidden beneath a shell or wings. Some arthropods, such as mites and most spiders, don't have distinct body segments.

Molting

An arthropod exoskeleton can't grow, as our skin and bones can, so an arthropod doesn't gradually get larger and larger as it gets older. Instead, it regularly sheds its old "skin" and suddenly gets a new one. This is called **molting**, and here's how it works. First, a new exoskeleton begins to form underneath the old one. The muscles and nerves that were attached to the original exoskeleton become attached to the new one. For a while, the animal is actually covered by two "skins", one inside the other. Eventually, the old exoskeleton splits and the animal crawls out of it. The new exoskeleton is soft and stretchy at first. The

animal's body, which had been tightly packed in the old exoskeleton, is now able to expand, and the exoskeleton expands with it. As the animal takes in air or water its new skin may get even larger. Soon, however, the new exoskeleton dries and hardens. After that it can't grow anymore, and the animal will stay at its new size until the next molt.

These animals have different diets and live in different environments, but they are all arthropods. Can you see anything that they have in common?

The green crab on the left recently molted. The much smaller exoskeleton it emerged from is on the right. When a crab molts, its exoskeleton splits open along the back and sides and the crab backs out of it.

Who's Who Among the Arthropods

Over one million different kinds of animals are known to live on our planet, and about three-quarters of them are arthropods! Scientists divide the animals in the phylum Arthropoda into nine or ten classes. This book will help you get acquainted with six of those classes.

Characteristics of some arthropod classes

THE CENTIPEDES — CLASS CHILOPODA

Centipedes have fangs and a poisonous bite, and most are active predators. Adults have 15–20 pairs of legs, with one pair growing from each body segment. Centipedes have one pair of antennae, three pairs of jaws, and **simple eyes** that don't form images. Their bodies are covered with a smooth, flexible material.

THE MILLIPEDES — CLASS DIPLOPODA

Most millipedes have long, worm-like bodies covered with a tough exoskeleton, but a few are soft-bodied. Adults have between 13 and 100 pairs of legs, depending on the species. Two pairs of legs grow from each **body ring** (each ring is made up of two segments). Millipedes have one pair of antennae on their heads and one pair of jaws. Most millipedes are scavengers.

CRUSTACEANS — CLASS CRUSTACEA

Most crustaceans live in water, but a few, like the pillbugs, live on land. Some crustaceans breathe through gills, but others get oxygen directly through the surface of their bodies.

Many crustaceans use both gills and body surfaces to breathe. Most crustaceans have two pair of antennae in front of their mouths and at least three pairs of jaws. Lobsters, crabs, shrimp, pillbugs, and barnacles are all crustaceans.

8

THE INSECTS —
CLASS INSECTA

An insect's body has three major parts: a head, a middle section called the **thorax**, and an abdomen. (It is not always easy to distinguish these parts.) A pair of antennae grow on the head, and three pairs of legs grow from the thorax. Many adult insects have wings, and most have large **compound eyes** in addition to simple eyes. Beetles, flies, and cicadas are all insects.

SPIDERS AND
THEIR RELATIVES —
CLASS ARACHNIDA

Arachnids have two main body parts: a **fused** or joined head and thorax, called the **cephalothorax**, and an abdomen. Most have four pairs of legs and simple eyes. They do not have antennae. Some arachnids breathe through special organs called **book lungs**, while others get oxygen directly through their body surfaces or through special tubes. Most arachnids prey on other arthropods, but only a few can chew solid food. The rest pour digestive enzymes onto their prey and then suck up the liquid that results.

HORSESHOE CRABS —
CLASS MEROSTOMATA

Horseshoe crabs have a flattened, horseshoe-shaped cephalothorax and an abdomen that ends in a long, spine-like tail. They have both compound and simple eyes. They also have five pairs of walking legs. In young crabs and in females, the first pair of walking legs end in pincers. In males they look more like boxing gloves or mittens. There are only five living species of horseshoe crabs.

Classification

There are different ways to **classify**, or group, the thousands of kinds of arthropods that live on our planet. Sometimes it is useful to group together those that live in a particular place, or those that have a certain way of moving or feeding. (For instance, lice, ticks, many mites, and some wasps are **parasites**; they live in or on the bodies of other living animals. Most millipedes, however, are **scavengers**; they eat dead plants.) Other times, it is helpful to group animals based on the way their bodies look and work, and on their evo-

Taxonomy

PHYLUM: *Arthropoda (animals with paired, jointed legs and a hard exoskeleton)*
CLASS: *Insecta (the insects)*
ORDER: *Orthoptera (crickets, grasshoppers, and their relatives)*
GENUS: *Dissosteira*
SPECIES: *Dissosteira carolina (carolina grasshopper)*

lutionary history. Scientists pay particular attention to body plan and evolutionary history in deciding which animals to group together in the phylum Arthropoda.

Any phylum can be further divided. Scientists sort the animals in a phylum into **classes**, then divide each class into **orders**. Each order is again divided into families, and families are further divided into **genera**. Each time a division is made, the animals that are most closely related are grouped together. Finally, animals are sorted into distinct **species**, or kinds, and each species is assigned a special, two-part Latin name. Classifying animals is called **taxonomy**. If you are interested in the way scientists classify the animals in this book, look for the Taxonomy boxes on different pages, such as this one for the carolina grasshopper.

INDOORS

You don't have to travel to exotic places to study arthropods. In fact, you don't even need to leave home. Just take a good look around your bedroom, bathroom, kitchen, or basement. Most likely, a few fruit flies, spiders, cockroaches, centipedes and other fascinating arthropods have already moved in with you!

Window watching

Get in the habit of checking your windows for arthropods. Insects that have accidentally wandered into your home may be attracted to a sunny window as they look for a way back out. You may find stout-legged jumping spiders patrolling sills and screens in search of prey, while their web-spinning cousins build silken insect-traps across a corner.

Check your windows at night as well as during the day. No one is sure exactly why, but many night-flying insects are attracted to bright lights. When it is dark outside and you have lights on indoors, look to see if any insects are banging against your windows. Beetles and moths will probably be among your visitors. During the summer, katydids may also perch on your screen. If you are lucky, you may even see a polyphemus or cecropia moth, or one of the other beautiful members of the giant silk moth family.

Getting to know your cobwebs

The cobwebs people vacuum from their ceilings and walls are made by spiders. Next time you spot a cobweb, stop and take a good look at it. Different kinds of spiders make different types of webs, and you may discover several species living in one room. (You will often find a spider hanging from the middle of its web or resting nearby.)

Look for round, silken egg sacs, as well as spiders, in the webs you find. Female spiders spin these protective sacs around their eggs. The eggs of many species hatch while they are still inside the sac, and the tiny spiders feed on one another until it is time for them to emerge. Eventually, the baby spiders that are left leave the sac and find places to spin webs of their own.

Down in the cellar

Camel crickets live in dark, moist places. They are insects, as are other crickets. You can find them outdoors under rocks and logs and in caves. Indoors, a damp cellar is a good place to look. You can recognize camel crickets by their extremely long hind legs and antennae. Often, their antennae are even longer then their bodies, and they touch, or nearly touch, each other at their base between the cricket's eyes. Camel crickets have arched backs and no wings.

Camel crickets are common throughout the United States. You may never have seen one, though, because they are usually active at night. If you want to find them, you may have to schedule some late-evening trips to the basement. If they scurry away when you flick on the lights, try looking for them with a flashlight. If they flee from the

These spider egg cases are already hatching—you can see dozens of baby spiders hanging in their mother's web outside.

Camel cricket

flashlight as well, fasten red cellophane over the end. (Many nocturnal animals can be observed with a red light. It seems that they don't see colors at the red end of the spectrum as well as we do, so the red light doesn't bother them.)

You can keep camel crickets in a terrarium with a layer of sand or soil in it. Fit it with a lid and add a few rocks, cardboard tubes, or other objects for them to crawl in or under. Camel crickets are scavengers and will eat nearly anything, from dead insects to dry dog food. Experiment to see which foods your crickets prefer. Use your flashlight or a lamp with a red bulb in it to observe them at night.

Upstairs

The house cricket, **Acheta domesticus**, may also share your home. House crickets thrive in warm climates. In the south they can live outdoors, but they can only survive a northern winter if they make their way into a warm building. House crickets didn't always live in this country, but were introduced from Europe. You can recognize them by their light brown color and the dark bands on their heads. Field crickets may also wander into your home. They look similar to house crickets, but they are dark brown or black. Both are easy to raise and interesting to watch.

Surrounded by Spiders

o one is sure how many different kinds of spiders live on Earth. More than 30,000 species have already been described, and unfamiliar ones keep turning up. Some scientists think that over 100,000 species of spiders actually exist. More than 14,000 individual spiders may inhabit a single acre of woodland, and four times as many can live in an acre of meadow.

Survey your spiders

Spiders live in all kinds of places. You can find them in tall weeds, on closely mowed lawns, and in tunnels in the ground. Many spiders build webs to catch prey in. Often, it is easier to spot a spider's web than to find the spider itself. Start looking for webs and spiders in your yard, schoolyard, or any other place you know well. You can survey the entire area, or mark off a small plot within it. Keep track of the different spiders and webs you find.

Don't forget to check the mailbox

Most people don't pay much attention to the spiders that live around them, and they certainly aren't thinking about spiders when they collect their daily mail. But some people do notice spiders, and have found that spiders live—of all places —in their mailboxes! This set a few people to wondering: were they in danger of encountering a poisonous spider when they picked up their mail?

Eric Edwards is a mailman. He is also a researcher with a particular interest in spiders. This put him in an ideal position to find out just what sort of spiders inhabit mailboxes. For three years, Edwards collected the spiders he found in, and on, the

Eric Edwards and his daughter, Emily, look for spiders in the woods behind their house.

mailboxes of Mashpee, Massachusetts. He identified each spider and kept track of where and when he found each one. His study revealed some fascinating things. For one thing, he found 158 different species of spiders in or on the mailboxes he looked at. Although black widows are known to live in the area, none showed up in the boxes. Further, the spiders Edwards found seemed to be doing different things. Some seemed to be looking for a mate, while others were **ballooning**, or para-chuting along on strands of silk, in search of places to build their webs. Still others were permanent resi-

dents; they actually lived inside the mailboxes.

It turns out that not all mailboxes are equal from a spider's point of view. Edwards found fewer spiders on the outside of mailboxes that were painted white than he did on boxes that were unpainted or paint-ed black. And, although spiders often tucked themselves into crevices in plastic mailboxes to molt, on the whole they were more com-mon in and on metal boxes than on plastic ones. Some species seemed to prefer particular parts of the mail-box. Others were more flexible and built webs in many different places.

The daddy longlegs

Daddy longlegs are common arachnids that are often mistaken for spiders. But look closely at the next one you catch, and you'll notice features that set it apart from spiders. A daddy longlegs' head blends right into its body, while a spider's head is distinct, connected to its body by a thin stalk. A daddy longlegs has just two eyes while most spiders have eight. Researchers have also learned that if a daddy longlegs loses one of its long, delicate legs, it cannot grow another. Spiders, on the other hand, can **regenerate** a missing leg. Daddy longlegs belong to the order *Opiliones*, or "harvestmen." They eat live insects, dead animals, and plants.

A female nursery web spider carries her egg sacs with her until close to hatching time. Then she fastens some leaves together like a protective roof and stands guard near her nursery.

Spider safety

Nearly all spiders produce poison that can paralyze the insects and other small animals they prey on, but only a few make poison that is dangerous to humans. One is the brown recluse, *Loxosceles reclusa*, and another is the female black widow, *Latrodectus mactans*. Although it is unusual for any spider, including a widow or recluse, to bite a person, it is a good idea to find out if there are any potentially dangerous spiders in your area. If there are, learn to recognize them and make sure not to handle one if you see it. Some people are extra sensitive to all spider venom, just as some people are allergic to bee stings. So if you want to catch a non-poisonous spider, gently scoop it up with a paper cup or plastic container.

Taxonomy

PHYLUM: *Arthropoda*
CLASS: *Arachnida (arthropods with four pairs of legs and two body parts—spiders, mites, scorpions, pseudoscorpions, harvestmen, etc.)*
ORDER: *Araneae (spiders) Some families: Araneidae (orb weavers. Includes Argiope aurantia; the black and yellow argiope) Agelenidae (funnel weavers) Pisauridae (nursery web spiders and fishing spiders) Salticidae (jumping spiders)*
ORDER: *Opiliones (harvestmen)*
FAMILY: *Phalangiidae (daddy longlegs)*

Jumping spiders are active during the day. Instead of trapping their prey in a web, they pounce right on it. Here, one is caught in mid-pounce on a garden rose.

IN THE GARDEN

Flower and vegetable gardens are good places to find spiders, insects, and other arthropods. If you don't have a garden yourself, visit a neighbor's garden, or go to a local farm, park, or community garden. You will have the best luck finding arthropods in gardens that are not sprayed with pesticides, so make sure to ask about this. You'll also be taking care of yourself, because pesticides can be harmful to humans as well as to weeds and bugs.

Where to look

Some arthropods will be easy to find. You may see bees flying from flower to flower, or grasshoppers leaping out of your way as you walk along the garden path. You will have to look more closely to find others. Some arthropods cling to plant stems or the undersides of leaves. Still others may be the same color as the plants they are on, making them difficult to spot.

Arthropods make changes in a garden. They often leave traces that tell you where they've been and what they've been doing, such as:
- holes nibbled in leaves or vegetables
- squiggly pathways or tunnels that have been "mined" in leaves
- eggs, empty eggshells, or cocoons
- spider webs

Try looking for arthropods:
- on and under garden mulch
- on and under leaves
- along stems
- in and on flowers
- on the ground

The holes in the leaves of this broccoli plant were probably nibbled by a green caterpillar, the larva of the cabbage white butterfly.

Garden Beetles

Asparagus beetles live in the eastern United States. Look for them on asparagus plants, their sole source of food. Adult beetles are small, but their bright colors make them stand out. Common asparagus beetles have dark wings with yellowish spots, and spotted asparagus beetles are red with black spots. You'll have to look hard to find the larvae, whose dark blue-green bodies match the asparagus almost perfectly.

Most gardeners like having ladybugs around, because they eat aphids and other small, soft-bodied insects that can damage plants. Even though most people call them "bugs," scientists group these insects with the Coleoptera, or beetles, because they have a hard, shiny covering over their wings, and chewing mouthparts. There are about 400 different species of ladybugs in North America; many are orange or yellow with black spots.

Potato Beetles

Visit any garden where potatoes are growing, and you are likely to find Colorado potato beetles nibbling on their leaves. You can recognize adult beetles by their black and yellow stripes. The larvae, or young beetles, are orange with rows of black dots along their sides. You may also find potato beetles on eggplants, peppers, tomatoes, and other plants that are closely related to potatoes.

Adult potato beetles are about 1/4 inch long and nearly as wide.

Potato beetle history

Colorado potato beetles, *Leptinotarsa decemlineata,* are native to the United States. They originally lived near the Rocky Mountains, where they fed on nightshade, sandburr and other wild members of the potato family. Gradually, they also began to eat the cultivated potatoes of people who settled and farmed in the area. In the mid-1800s, these beetles began expanding their **range**, moving from potato patch to potato patch across the country. Today, they can be found in every state except California, Nevada, Alaska, and Hawaii.

This potato patch has fed a lot of Colorado potato beetles, but it may not produce a good crop for the people who planted it!

Potato pests

In the eastern United States, the Colorado potato beetle is a serious agricultural pest. In the spring, adult beetles emerge from a long winter underground and begin eating potato leaves and stems. They mate and the females lay clusters of bright yellow eggs on the potato leaves. Soon, scores of newly hatched larvae join their feasting parents. Since potato plants need their leaves in order to grow, a potato patch that is heavily infested with beetles will not produce a good crop.

For many years, farmers and gardeners have tried to limit the damage done by the Colorado potato beetle by spraying **insecticides** on their plants. For a while this seemed to solve the problem, but eventually, it became clear that this caused problems as well. Many insecticides poisoned not only pests but also helpful insects, birds, and other animals. In addition, Colorado potato beetles began to show **resistance** to many of the chemicals that formerly killed them. This resistance developed because even the most effective sprays did not poison every beetle in a field. The few beetles that managed to survive would mate and produce young that often inherited their parents' ability to tolerate particular poisons. Over time, the potato beetle population in the eastern United States has shifted from one that was highly susceptible to insecticides to one that is now fairly tolerant of them.

*Potato beetle larvae feed on potato leaves for two to three weeks, then crawl underground to **pupate**, or transform into adults.*

Searching for new solutions

Potato beetles do have a few natural enemies. One is a fungus called *Beaveria bassiana.* This fungus lives in the soil, where it produces tiny seed-like **fruiting bodies** called conidia. If a potato beetle comes into contact with a conidia, the conidia will begin to grow on the beetle's body. Actually, the conidia grows right into the beetle's body, producing thread-like structures that spread through its blood and kill it.

Researchers hope to use *B. bassiana* to develop effective and environmentally sound ways to control the potato beetle. But their work is complicated by the fact that many potato growers are plagued not only by the potato beetle, but also by a plant disease called **late blight**. Late blight is caused by another fungus, and some growers combat it by spraying their crops with **fungicides**, chemicals that kill fungi. If growers continue to use fungicides to control late blight, can they also use *B. bassiana* to kill potato beetles? Or will the fungicides that kill the late blight fungus destroy the *B. bassiana* as well?

One researcher's work

Jenny Jaros is trying to answer these questions by studying the ways different fungicides affect *B. bassiana.* Part of her work goes on in the laboratory. There, she checks to see whether potato beetle larvae that have been exposed to *B. bassiana* alone are infected at the same rate as larvae that have been exposed to both *B. bassiana* and fungicides. The other part of her work is outdoors, because pesticides don't always behave the same way in the field as they do in the lab. Jaros learns how pesticides interact outdoors by spraying them in different combina-

tions. She applies *B. bassiana* alone to some potato plots, and treats others with both *B. bassiana* and various fungicides. Five days later, she goes back to each plot and counts the number of adult beetles and larvae. She also examines the larvae to see how many are infected with *B. bassiana.* Jaros hopes to find a fungicide that won't kill the *B. bassiana,* while still stopping the late blight fungus.

Taxonomy

CLASS: *Insecta (the insects)*
ORDER: *Coleoptera (the beetles)*
FAMILY: *Chrysomelidae (leaf beetles)*
GENUS AND SPECIES: *Leptinotarsa decemlineata*

Adult and larval potato beetles feeding on potato leaves.

IN THE FIELD

Many kinds of arthropods live in open fields. If you live near a field, plan to visit it often. Go at different times of day and during different seasons. Animals that are scarce or hard to find at one time may be easy to find at another.

Things to bring

Wood tick

- A magnifying glass will help you get a close look at any tiny arthropods you find.
- A net can help you catch insects that are hidden in tall weeds, or that fly away before you can get a close look at them.
- A coffee can or plastic container will temporarily hold arthropods while you watch them.
- A garden trowel is useful if you want to search for soil dwellers.
- A notebook and pencil will allow you to record what you see.
- Shoes, socks and long pants will protect you from thorns, prickers, bites, and stings.

A few arthropods you might find

Aphids and thornhoppers are small insects that suck juice from plant stems. As they eat, they secrete a liquid waste called honeydew. You may see ants come and collect the honeydew, as it is sugary and they use it for food.

In the summer, you will probably hear grasshoppers as well as see them. The sounds you hear are mating calls, and in most cases, it is the adult males that make them. Adult grasshoppers usually have long wings. The nymphs, or young, hatch without wings and gradually develop them.

Earwigs sometimes seek shelter in the cracks and crevices formed by plant leaves.

Wood ticks are parasites of large mammals. When a deer, dog, or person brushes against the plant a wood tick is resting on, the tick hops on board, sticks its specialized mouthparts through the mammal's skin, and begins to suck blood. As it feeds, its expandable body swells until it is several times its pre-meal size. When it has drunk its fill, the tick withdraws its mouthparts and drops off. It may not eat again for many months.

Avoiding tick bites

Even though tick bites are painless, it is important to try to avoid them, because some ticks carry germs that can spread disease. Rocky Mountain spotted fever and Lyme disease are both carried to people by ticks. To avoid tick bites, wear long pants when exploring fields. Tuck your pant-legs into your socks to keep ticks from crawling up your leg. Long-sleeved shirts and turned-up collars also help. If you wear light-colored clothing instead of dark, it's easier to see any ticks that have landed on you. Check yourself, or have a friend check you, whenever you leave a tick-infested area, and brush off any that you find. Wood ticks are easy to spot,

but you'll have to look closely to find the tiny deer ticks that spread Lyme disease. They are as small as a poppy seed!

Taxonomy

Aphids and thornhoppers:
  CLASS: **Insecta**
  ORDER: **Homoptera**
Earwigs:
  CLASS: **Insecta**
  ORDER: **Dermaptera**
Grasshoppers:
  CLASS: **Insecta**
  ORDER: **Orthoptera**
Ticks:
  CLASS: **Arachnida**
  ORDER: **Acari**

19

Praying Mantids

Praying mantids live in fields, gardens, vacant lots, and other open place where they can find plants to climb on and insects to eat. Depending on the species, a full-grown mantis may be anywhere from two to five inches long. Even so, you may have to look hard to find one. Mantids are green or light brown and tend to blend in with the plants they walk among.

This mantis may keep perfectly still, but will strike if another insect comes near enough.

Mantis life

Young mantids, called **nymphs**, hatch from eggs. Nymphs look like small versions of their parents, except that they lack wings. From the start they are hunters, and will eat any insects they are able to catch. A mantis stands extremely still when it hunts, holding its front legs up as if praying. It seems to be doing nothing, but actually it is keeping a sharp look-out for insects. If one happens to wander near, the mantis shoots out its spiny forelegs, both grabbing and stabbing its prey. Mantis nymphs go through several molts before reaching their full size. As they grow, they are able to handle larger and larger insects. There have even been reports of mantids grabbing toads, shrews, and small birds!

Mantis love

In cool climates, mantids mate during the summer and early fall. Afterwards, the females lay between 40 and 500 eggs in a frothy substance that hardens into a protective egg case. Though the females die when cold weather hits, their eggs can withstand the winter. Male mantids may not even live to see the winter, for they are often devoured by their mates while mating, or just after. This is a gruesome practice from a human standpoint, but scientists think it may actually serve an important purpose for mantids. It could be that females who get a large, protein-rich meal—such as a male mantid—during or just after mating are able to lay more eggs than they otherwise could. If so, a mated pair that "sacrifices" the male may have a better chance of producing young.

Mantis egg case

Native or import

Many of our most familiar mantids are actually **introduced species**. That is, they did not originally live here, but eggs or adults were imported by people. For instance, the European mantis was accidentally sent from Europe to New York State on plants that were shipped to a nursery in 1899. This species now ranges throughout the northeast and into Canada. The Carolina mantis, on the other hand, is a **native species**. It can be found in many southeastern states. Introduced species are often considered pests, but many people appreciate the European and Chinese mantids because they eat other insects that are even more pesty.

Raising mantids

Mantids are fascinating to watch, and easy to raise if you keep their needs and habits in mind.

Housing: An old fish tank or a gallon glass jar makes a good mantis cage. Make a lid out of window screen or mosquito netting. Put a little dirt in the bottom of the cage and add a clump of weeds or grass to give your mantis something to climb on. You can spray a little water on the weeds and soil from time to time, but take care not to create a soggy, humid environment in the cage.

Numbers: Mantids are solitary animals, so keep only one in each cage.

You can make a temporary home for a mantid from an old fish tank or a simple gallon jar.

If you crowd them, they are likely to eat one another.

Food and Water: Keep your mantid supplied with live insects to eat. Catch insects outside or buy live crickets at a pet store that sells them for lizard food.

Hatching your own: If you find a mantis egg case that has not yet hatched, you may want to bring it home and keep it until it does. Carry it home, plant stem and all, since trying to remove it from the stem might damage it. If you live where winters are cool, keep the egg case in your refrigerator so it does not hatch right away. Otherwise you'll be overrun with baby mantids at a time of year when it is almost impossible to find food for them! In late spring, when the weather is warm and you are finding lots of insects outdoors, move the egg case out of the refrigerator and into a jar with a screen lid. When the new mantids emerge, keep a few to raise and let the rest go. Newly hatched mantids are tiny, and they will need tiny food. Try miniature prey, like aphids and fruit flies. As they grow, you can add larger insects to their diet.

Mail-order mantids: If you can't find a mantis, order an egg case from one of the supply companies listed on page 62. Check to see if you can get one from a species that lives wild in your area. If you can't, you'll need to make sure you don't let your hatchlings loose outdoors.

Flies

 Many people use the word "fly" to refer to that buzzing indoor pest, the housefly. Scientists often use the term more broadly, to mean any one of more than 80,000 species of flies, mosquitoes, midges, and gnats that make up the insect order **Diptera**. Spend some time getting to know the flies in your kitchen, garden, or classroom. They are bound to entertain and amaze you as well as sometimes annoy you.

This robber fly is laying eggs. Notice the long proboscis, bulging eyes and hairy face characteristic of the robber flies.

Robber flies

Robber flies are also called assassin flies, for they are dramatic and capable hunters. They will eat flies, beetles, bees, and even grasshoppers, dragonflies, and other insects larger than themselves. A robber fly usually perches on a leaf, weed, or twig to watch for food. When something flies or moves nearby, the robber quickly darts out to investigate. Sometimes, on closer inspection, it finds that the "prey" is nothing other than a falling flower petal or bit of debris. When the object really is a prey animal, the robber fly will try to intercept it and scoop it up in its strong, bristly legs.

Once the robber fly has captured an insect, it stabs its prey with a sharp, beak-like mouthpart called the **proboscis**. The proboscis injects a toxic saliva that paralyzes the insect, making it easier for the robber fly to carry it back to its perch. Once settled, the robber fly begins to feed on its prey, sucking out the body juices with the proboscis.

Courting

Although hunting is one of the robber fly's most obvious behaviors, you may also see them courting, mating, or laying eggs. In some species, a male will court a female by flying near her and buzzing his wings at different pitches. Males and females may also display patches of silvery hair to one another. Afterwards, the female robber fly lays her eggs. The larvae that hatch out will live in or near the ground, eating any live insects that they can catch.

Mating flies

How to recognize a robber fly

Robber flies are found throughout the world, and there are about 900 species in North America alone! As you try to distinguish them from other kinds of flies and insects, pay attention to their behavior as well as their appearance. Robber flies have

This hover fly is helping the flower as well as feeding itself, by moving pollen from one flower to the next.

Taxonomy

CLASS: *Insecta*
ORDER: *Diptera (flies, gnats, mosquitoes, and relatives)*
SOME FAMILIES:
Culicidae (mosquitoes)
Simuliidae (black flies)
Tabanidae (horse flies, green flies, and deer flies)
Syrphidae (flower flies)
Muscidae (house flies)
Asilidae (robber flies)

round, bulging eyes that are set wide apart on their heads. Their faces are hairy, and have a sharp, forward-pointing proboscis. Many have long, slender bodies, but some are stout and hairy all over and look like bees. Some robber flies are black or brown, while others have yellow or reddish markings. In general, a robber fly's hunting technique of perching, watching, and darting out to snatch its prey will help you tell it apart from many other similar-looking insects.

Hover flies

In order for flowering plants to produce fruit and seeds, they must be **pollinated**. Tiny grains of pollen must be moved from one part of a flower

(the anther) to another (the stigma), and usually from one flower to another as well. Wind moves some pollen around, but most plants depend on insects to pollinate them.

Hover flies are important pollinators. They feed on nectar from flowers. While feeding, they often brush against a flower and get pollen on their legs and bodies. They carry this pollen to the next flower they feed at. If a little rubs off on a flower of the right species, that flower may be pollinated. Look for hover flies wherever you see flowers in bloom.

Hover fly larvae live in many places. Some can be found on leaves, eating aphids. Others live in stagnant pools of water, manure, rotting logs, or wasp nests. Most adult

hover flies are 3/8 to 3/4 inch long. Many species look quite a bit like wasps or bees, and make a bee-like buzzing sound when they fly. They have no stingers and cannot bite you, so you can observe them closely and handle them without protection.

Telling the flies from the bees

Many hover flies and some robber flies look a lot like bees or wasps. With practice, you can learn to tell them apart. See the table at left for some differences to remember.

In addition, hover flies can hold themselves absolutely still in midair when they hover; bees and wasps bob up and down a bit when they hover.

FLIES HAVE:	BEES AND WASPS HAVE:
• one pair of flying wings • short inconspicuous antennae • large eyes • piercing or sponging mouthparts	• two pairs of flying wings • longer antennae • medium-sized eyes • chewing mouthparts • stingers

Raising a Monarch

he monarch, *Danaeus plexippus*, is a large, slow-flying, black and orange butterfly. It is easy to raise a monarch butterfly from an egg or caterpillar that you find outside. If you live in the southern United States, start looking for them in March or April. Further north, you probably won't spot any until May, June, or even later.

Housing and care

An old fish tank, a gallon glass jar, or a cage made from a piece of wire screening and two round cake pans will make a fine temporary home for your monarch. You can even use a cardboard box with a screen or plastic wrap window taped on one side. If your container is glass or smooth plastic, drape a piece of cheesecloth or netting along one side to give your caterpillar— and eventually your butterfly—something to cling to. Cheesecloth or netting can also be used to make a lid. Just cut out a piece a little larger than the opening of your container and fasten it on with a rubber band.

You will need to keep your caterpillar supplied with fresh milkweed to eat. Place a milkweed stalk in a small jar of water and cover the opening with foil or plastic so that your caterpillar does not fall in and drown. Replace the milkweed whenever the leaves begin to look dry or shriveled, or when your caterpillar has eaten most of them. Try to get young, tender leaves, since they are the easiest to chew.

A large caterpillar will eat lots of leaves, and produce plenty of waste, or **frass**. When its cage needs cleaning, simply wipe the frass out with a tissue or paper towel.

Find some milkweed

If you want to find a monarch egg or caterpillar, you will first need to find some milkweed. Monarch caterpillars are picky eaters—they will only eat leaves of the common milkweed, *Ascelpias syriaca,* and its close relatives. A female monarch butterfly cements each of her eggs to the underside of a milkweed leaf so that each new caterpillar hatches right on its food.

Look for milkweed in fields, vacant lots, and along roadsides. In the spring you can recognize the common milkweed by the furry undersides of its oblong leaves and by the sticky white sap that oozes out if you pick a leaf or tear it. In the summer, you'll also notice large clusters of pink flowers. Once you have found a milkweed plant, check the underside of each leaf. If you find a tiny egg or a striped caterpillar, take it home. Don't try to remove the egg from the leaf. Simply cut the stem of the milkweed with a knife or scissors, then carry the plant home with the egg still in place.

Things to look for

You can expect a monarch egg to hatch within four days. The tiny caterpillar that emerges will eat its eggshell, and then will start eating the milkweed. Soon it will molt and grow.

Over the next ten days or so, the caterpillar will go through several more cycles of eating, molting, and growing. Long black antennae will develop on its head, and shorter, antenna-like stalks will grow near its rear end. When the caterpillar eats, you may be able to get a good look at its legs and mouthparts, and see how it uses them. Keep track of how much milkweed you put in the cage, and try to figure out how much your caterpillar eats in a day.

When the caterpillar is about 10–14 days old, it will stop eating. It may seem sick, but actually, it is preparing for a special molt. You may see it spin a small web of silk under a milkweed leaf or on the top of the cage. Or you may notice that it is hanging upside-down from the web with its body curved like the letter **J**. Keep an eye on it at this point, so you can watch the amazing change that happens next.

The upside-down caterpillar will start to wriggle. Finally, its skin will split open and you will see that a **chrysalis** has formed underneath it. At first, the chrysalis will look bright green, but over the next 9–15 days it will turn clear. As it changes, you will be able to see the wings of the butterfly that is developing inside.

Finally, the chrysalis will split open and a damp, crumpled butterfly will crawl out. Over the next hour or two, you can watch it pump fluid into its wings. When the wings look firm and dry, the monarch is ready to fly and you can let it go.

Plant a Garden for Butterflies

 f you want to attract butterflies to your home or school, plant a garden for them. Choose plants that provide adult butterflies with **nectar** to drink, and caterpillars with the proper leaves to chew on.

Plan before you plant

Before you actually plant your garden, try to find out what kinds of butterflies live near you, and what plants they use for food. Spend some time outside looking for butterflies and caterpillars, and keep track of the plants they visit. If you don't know the names of the butterflies and plants you see, describe and sketch them in a notebook. Later, you can compare your notes with the descriptions in a field guide, or show them to a knowledgeable gardener or insect-lover. Once you know that a particular plant attracts butterflies, you can put it on the list of possible species to plant in your garden.

Plant a bit of baby food

Though an adult butterfly will drink nectar from many different flowers, its larvae, or caterpillars, usually need a particular type of leaf to eat. Monarch larvae, for example, feed on milkweed, while black swallowtail caterpillars eat carrots, parsley, and Queen Anne's lace. If you want butterflies to lay their eggs in your garden as well as sip nectar there, plant some flowers, shrubs or vegetables that provide food for their young. Field guides, butterfly books, and your own observations will help you figure out which food plants to try out in your garden.

Go native

Gardeners often grow **cultivated** plants. These have been developed by plant breeders to produce many large vegetables or showy blossoms. Gardeners also tend to plant species that did not originally live in the area where they garden. A New England garden may include poppies that grow wild in California or China, irises from Siberia, and cosmos from Mexico. But people who care about butterflies and other arthropods

This tiger swallowtail butterfly will lay its eggs on the leaves of birch, cherry, or ash trees.

believe that it's important to plant many native species in a garden. This is because the plants and animals that naturally **evolved** together in a particular region depend on one another. Monarch butterflies *need* milkweed—without it they cannot produce a new generation of butterflies. And milkweed, in turn, depends on the monarch and many other insects to pollinate it. When we change natural areas to make room for roads and lawns, we eliminate places where butterflies can find food and lay eggs. Replanting native species in areas where they have been destroyed can help butterflies survive.

Planting and tending

If you already have a garden at home or school, you can convert it into a butterfly garden by adding some new plants. If you are starting from scratch, choose a sunny spot that is protected from strong winds. Prepare the soil by removing grass and weeds, and loosening it with a

Bee balm, Monarda didyma, *is visited by hummingbirds as well as butterflies. It is native from New York to Minnesota and south.*

garden fork or spade. If the soil is poor, you can add peat moss or rotted manure. Once the soil is ready, add your plants. Spread leaf litter or rotted compost around the base of your plants, to shelter larvae and **pupae**. And keep your garden pesticide-free! Weed and insect killers can be unhealthy for you, and may kill the animals you are trying to attract and observe.

If you don't have room for a garden

Plant a few flowers, herbs, or vegetables that attract butterflies in a large pot or window box. Or see if there is a community garden in your neighborhood that you can share. If you can't find a place to make a garden, then find a place to visit one. Many communities have botanical gardens, parks, and other areas that are planted with flowers.

Various species of goldenrod, Solidago spp., *grow in different parts of North America. Goldenrod is an important food source for butterflies during the late summer and early fall, when most other flowers have **gone to seed**.*

Queen Anne's lace, Daucus carota, *or wild carrot, was brought to America by colonists and now grows wild in many places. It is a food plant for black swallowtail caterpillars.*

More than 100 species of milkweed grow naturally in North America. The beautiful butterfly weed, Asclepias tuberosa, *is a favorite with gardeners.*

Finding native plants

It is tempting to dig up wildflowers wherever you find them, but this is not the best way to acquire plants for your garden! You might unknowingly take plants that are rare, or transplant flowers that will not thrive in their new home. Instead, buy native plants at a nursery, or start your own from seeds. If you call or write to them, the National Wildflower Research Center (2600 FM 973 North, Austin TX 78725, (512) 929-3600) can help you figure out what to plant in your area. For $3.50, you can also buy a guide to native plants from The Soil Conservation Society of America (7515 NE. Ankeny Road, Ankeny IA 50021, (515) 289–2331). And if you want to find the botanical club or native plant society nearest to you, contact the New England Wildflower Society at the Garden in the Woods, Hemenway Road, Framingham, MA 01701, (508) 877-7630).

Butterfly Watching

If you have a butterfly garden, you will want to spend time observing the caterpillars, butterflies, and moths in it. There are plenty of other places to watch butterflies as well. Look for them in fields and meadows, parks, woodlands, and along roads. You may even find them around puddles, piles of manure or sawdust, rotten fruit, and dead animals.

What to bring

Patience and persistence are the best things to bring when you go butterfly-watching. Butterflies do not appear on demand, and you may have to make several trips to a garden or weedy lot before you see any. You may want to carry binoculars, a hand lens, and a notebook on your expeditions. You may also want to bring a field guide to help you identify unfamiliar species.

Butterfly behavior

Once you find a butterfly, see what you can learn about its habits and behavior. The following are some of the things butterflies do that you may notice:

You can record your butterfly observations in a notebook.

Feeding: Every butterfly has a long, straw-like mouthpart called a proboscis for taking in food. Often, the **proboscis** stays curled up against the head. But when the butterfly lands on a flower, the proboscis uncoils and reaches down into the center of the flower where the **nectar** is stored. Look closely at a **nectaring** butterfly and you will usually be able to see its proboscis. Besides nectar, you may find butterflies sucking sap off a tree trunk or liquids from rotting fruit, manure, and dead animals.

Puddling: Butterflies sometimes gather to drink at puddles, along streams, or from damp soil. Researchers think that they collect salts and minerals from these sources.

Warming up: Butterflies are "cold blooded," that is, their body temperature changes with the temperature of the air around them. However, a butterfly cannot fly unless its wing muscles are between 75 and 100 degrees Fahrenheit. On cool days, butterflies have different ways of warming up enough to fly. Sometimes they **bask**, or rest on soil and other dark surfaces that absorb heat

from the sun. They spread out their wings and soak up heat from the warm soil, as well as whatever they can get from the sun itself. Some butterflies angle their bodies so that their wings catch the most possible sunlight. Some even vibrate or shiver their wings to warm them up.

Taking shelter: Butterflies, with their fragile wings, need to find shelter during rainstorms. They must also find safe places to rest at night, and may seek a shady spot when it is very hot and sunny. A few species even **overwinter** as adults, hibernating in cracks and crevices. At times when you don't see butterflies flying or feeding, try to find where they have taken cover. They may be clinging to the undersides of leaves, sitting on tree branches, or hidden under loose bark.

Taxonomy

CLASS: *Insecta (the insects)*
ORDER: *Lepidoptera (the "scale-winged" insects: butterflies, moths, and skippers).*

This large cecropia moth is laying her eggs. This is what they look like.

Courtship, mating, and egg laying: Sometimes you'll see two butterflies of the same species spiraling around each other, or chasing each other. These events often turn out to be **courtship flights**, which are sometimes followed by mating. You will know if two butterflies are mating if you see them with the tips of their abdomens joined together. After mating, the female looks for the proper plants on which to lay her eggs.

If you want to take a closer look

... but the butterfly keeps on moving around, use an insect net to catch it. You will occasionally be able to net a butterfly in flight, but it is easier to catch one that has landed. When you think you have one in your net, turn the handle so that the wire rim faces sideways and the fabric falls down to seal the opening. This will keep the butterfly from escaping. Next, place the rim on the ground, take hold of the small end of the net, and pull it up straight.

Your butterfly can then fly up into the small end and you can look at it through the mesh. If you want to watch it for a while or bring it indoors to identify it, gently transfer it to a large transparent container. When you are through, make sure you release the butterfly where you caught it.

29

Use a net to get a closer look at a butterfly. Handle your catch gently and release it where you found it.

AT THE GROCERY STORE

You may not have thought of looking for arthropods at the grocery store, but a grocery store with a good seafood department is one of the best places to get a look at a live lobster. In fact, you are far more likely to see a live lobster at the store than at the shore, because lobsters stay under the water and tend to move around at night. Fish markets, restaurants, and aquariums are also good places to look for lobsters. There are about 135 different kinds of lobsters in the world's oceans. The species sold in most North American markets is the northern lobster, *Homarus americanus*.

Lobster anatomy

When lots of lobsters are crowded together in a tank, it can be hard to see them clearly. Ask the person in charge of the tank if he or she will take one out for you to study. A grocery store lobster usually has a band around each of its two large claws, or chelipeds, so you can handle it without getting pinched. Wild lobsters use these claws to protect themselves and to catch prey. You'll notice that one claw is longer and more slender than the other. This claw, sometimes called the "ripper" or "pincher" claw, is lined with sharp teeth. It is used to grab prey and tear it apart. The short, wide claw is lined with bumps called tubercules, and is adapted for crushing.

You'll notice that your lobster has a hard shell covering its midsection, or thorax. If you turn it over, you can see that the legs that hold the large front claws are attached to the underside of the thorax. Four other pairs of jointed legs follow the large-clawed pair. They are used for walking, and the first two pair, which end in pincers, are also used to catch food. From underneath, you may also

be able to see the lobster's mouthparts, which are on its head, just in front of the first pair of legs.

A lobster's abdomen is divided into segments and ends in a tail fan, called the telson. Joints between each segment make the abdomen flexible. A lobster can even snap its telson under it and shoot backwards through the water. Small paddle-like swimmerets on the underside of some of the segments help the lobster swim forward. If you want to find out whether your lobster is male or female, check the pair of small appendages that grow from the underside of the first abdominal segment. In a female, they will be small and rather soft. In a male, they are hard and bony. The male's appendages transfer sperm to the female during mating. The telson can also help you determine the sex of your lobster: it is broader in females than in males.

Here is a northern lobster, showing the underside and back. Notice the five pairs of legs on the thorax, the mouthparts in front of them, and the small swimmerets along the abdomen.

Lobsters depend on their two sets of antennae for information about their environment.

How a lobster knows the world

A lobster's eyes probably don't see images, as human eyes do. In the dim light under sea, they work more like motion detectors. In the bright light of a grocery store or kitchen, they are useless. A lobster knows the world through touch and "smell." Like other crustaceans, a lobster has two pairs of antennae on its head. The long antennae are sensitive "feelers." The short pair detect chemicals, acting something like an underwater nose. Tiny hairs on the lobster's legs and feet also help it feel and "smell."

Growing up

The lobsters you see in the store may be five years old or even older. Each started out as a tiny egg no larger than the head of a pin. It was carried around on its mother's tail and swimmerets for 9–11 months until it hatched. A newly hatched lobster looks very different from the adults you see in the store. It has no claws, and instead of crawling on the ocean bottom, it floats near the surface of the water. After a few molts, it develops claws. By the fourth molt it is a little less than an inch long and looks like its older relatives. Lobsters can grow to be very large and very old. Some have reached lengths of 24, or even 34 inches and weighed in at 30–44 pounds. No one is sure how old these really big lobsters are, but some scientists think the oldest ones might be close to 100 years old!

Taxonomy

CLASS: *Crustacea*
ORDER: *Decapoda (decapods, including crabs, shrimp, lobsters and crayfish, all have ten legs)*
FAMILIES: *Homaridae or Nephrosidae (true lobsters)*
Palinuridae (spiny lobsters)
Scylliridae (slipper or Spanish lobsters)
Polychelidae (deep-sea lobsters)
GENUS AND SPECIES: *Homarus americanus*

In the wild

In the wild, northern lobsters are solitary animals. During the day they take shelter in crevices and burrows. At night they come out to look for food. They will eat live clams, starfish, and other prey, munch on algae and eelgrass, and scavenge dead animals from the ocean floor. Lobsters are territorial and will try to keep other lobsters away from their burrows. A large lobster will even eat a smaller one that strays too close. Bait stolen from lobster traps can also be an important part of a lobster's diet.

Many marine animals prey on young lobsters. Though a female can produce 10,000 or 20,000 eggs at a time, only 10–20 of the young that hatch will survive more than a month. Large lobsters have few predators other than people.

This is a drawing of the first larval stage of a lobster, right after it hatches. It is only one-third of an inch long.

Starting a Collection

You can learn more about the anatomy, identification, and classification of arthropods by studying preserved specimens. The suggestions below will help you start your own collection. Experienced collectors and field guides can help you develop it further.

Equipment

Before you start collecting specimens, gather the following equipment. You may already have some of it on hand, and you can order the rest from one of the biological supply houses listed on page 62.

- A net can help you catch live insects that are difficult to capture with your bare hands.
- A coffee can or plastic container with a tight-fitting lid can be used to contain and kill insects. It can also be used to hold other live arthropods.
- If you want to collect butterflies and other insects with large wings, you will need a **spreading board**.
- Pins are used to mount many insects. Use special **insect pins** rather than sewing pins, which are too thick and sometimes rust.
- Boxes with cork or foam lining the bottom are used to mount and store specimens. You can buy one or make one out of a cigar or shoe box.
- Alcohol will kill and preserve soft-bodied arthropods, such as spiders and mites. You can use rubbing alcohol from the drug store.
- Small glass jars or **vials** with tightly fitting lids will hold specimens preserved in alcohol.
- **Field guides** to insects, spiders, crabs, and other arthropods will help you identify the animals you collect. Many guides also give detailed instructions for preserving and displaying specimens.

Collecting

There are many ways to gather specimens for your collection. Beachcombing may yield crab claws or empty shells. Check on window sills and around street lamps and porch lights for dead moths, flies, and beetles. Catch live insects with your net, or pick them up with your fingers. You can even look through soil and dead leaves for tiny mites and other arthropods. Make sure to record the date and location where you collect each specimen, and make field notes about its behavior or appearance.

Killing and preserving live arthropods

There are two ways to kill live specimens. Put soft-bodied animals, like spiders, into a jar or vial of alcohol. The alcohol will both kill and preserve them. It may also change their color, so note the original color of the specimen before you preserve it. Most adult insects can be preserved without alcohol, since they will dry out once they are dead. Kill them by putting them in a can or plastic container in the freezer for a few hours. Then let them thaw out for a bit before handling them.

Pinning insects

Gently push a pin through the specimen's thorax in firmly into the bottom of the box. Glue very small specimens to a small triangle of paper and then pin the paper rather than the specimen. Make sure to pin your specimens soon after they are killed. If you wait too long, they will become brittle and will break when you try to pin them. You can leave them in an airtight container in the freezer if you think you won't be able to pin them right away. Also, if they do become brittle, you can make them soft again by putting them in a closed jar with a few drops of water in it for a day.

Spreading winged specimens

Butterflies, dragonflies, grasshoppers and many other insects are often displayed with one or both pairs of wings open. Spreading boards are used to prepare these specimens. You can find detailed directions for spreading insects in many field guides.

Crab claws and other beach finds

Rinse crab claws, molted crab and horseshoe crab shells, and other beach finds in cold water. If they remain dirty or smelly, scrub them gently with an old toothbrush, or soak them for an hour or two in water with a little bleach in it. Dry your specimens, then glue them to cardboard or put them in small cotton-filled boxes.

Labeling

Your collection will be most useful to yourself and others if you label each specimen. Cut labels out from heavy paper and size them to fit your display box or vial. Write the name of specimen, the date and place it was found, and the name of the person who found it on each label. Finished labels can be pinned on boxes or put right in the alcohol along with the specimen. For the latter, use either India ink or pencil so that your writing doesn't run in the alcohol.

Conservation

Here are some things you can do to conserve, or protect, arthropods while you build your collection:

- Collect arthropods that are already dead. Even if they are incomplete or damaged, you can still learn a lot from them.
- Collect the shed skins or exoskeletons that are left behind after an arthropod molts.
- Collect only one live specimen of any species (unless it is considered a pest in your area).
- Release any animals you catch that are rare, or uncommon in your area.
- Collect only as many animals as you can deal with. Remember, it takes time to preserve, display and label specimens, so collect just a few at a time.

FISHING FOR CRABS

Next time you go to the beach, plan to spend part of your time fishing. Some people like to catch bluefish, striped bass, and other good-tasting ocean fish, but if you are interested in arthropods, try fishing for crabs instead. You probably won't want to eat your catch, but you're bound to have fun watching it.

Things you'll need
- old sneakers or water shoes to protect your feet
- several long pieces of string
- a chicken wing for bait
- a plastic bucket

34

Directions
1. Find a safe, comfortable place to sit or stand.
2. Choose a piece of string long enough to reach down to the water from where you plan to fish. Then tie the chicken wing securely to one end of it.
3. Dangle the chicken wing in the water and wait for a while.
4. You may not feel it when a crab grabs onto the wing, so pull your bait up from time to time and take a look. Pull the wing up slowly, so that any hangers-on don't get washed off.
5. If there is a crab on your line, gently pull it off and put it in your bucket. Take care to keep your fingers away from its pinching claws! Or simply lower the crab, chicken wing and all, into your bucket for viewing.
6. When you are done observing your crab, let it go where you found it.
7. You can store your string and bait in the freezer for another day, or just throw them away.

Where to fish?
You can try fishing for crabs from a dock or from the water's edge. Choose a spot where the water is shallow and relatively calm. This is important for your own safety, as well as for your fishing success. If the waves are rough and the water

deep, any crabs you catch are likely to be knocked back into the water when you try to pull them out. More importantly, you might get swept into the water yourself. An adult should help you find a safe spot. Of course, you need to pick a spot where crabs live. If you don't know of one already, try fishing in tide pools and around rocks and clumps of seaweed, where the water is shallow and crabs can find shelter.

Nets and traps

In shallow water, you can scoop up crabs with a net. You can also collect crabs in special traps that look like cages. Put a bit of chicken or some other bait in the trap, then lower it into the water. Pull it up later to see if any crabs have found their way into it.

Substitute bait

Many crabs are scavengers, eating dead animals and whatever else they find lying around. They use their large pinching claws to pick up bits of food and pass it to their mouths. Crabs can see, but their ability to detect chemicals in the water is probably more important to them when it comes to finding food. A crab that finds your chicken wing has "smelled" or "tasted" it underwater. If you don't happen to have a chicken wing on hand, you can try catching crabs with another kind of bait—perhaps a bit of hot dog or a piece of ham from a sandwich. Just be aware that these foods are more difficult to secure to a fishing line.

All Kinds of Crabs

If you spend time exploring the coast, you are bound to find crabs, and probably more than one kind. Like lobsters, shrimp and crayfish, crabs are decapods. "Decapod" means "ten-footed," and decapod crustaceans have five pairs of legs, including the front pair which often have large claws. A hard shell called the carapace covers the fused head and thorax of crabs.

Colorful crabs

The blue crab, *Callinectes sapidus*, can be found in bays, **tidal creeks**, and mud flats. Sometimes they even move upriver into fresh water. You might see one swimming in the water with its paddle-shaped hind legs, or discover one hiding in the mud.

You can recognize a blue crab by the shape of its carapace, which is about twice as wide as it is long and has a pointed spine on each side. One front claw is often larger or thicker than the other. Each "finger" of the claw is lined with sharp, tooth-like points that help the crab keep a tight grip on live prey and scavenged meals. Male crabs have blue claws and females have red ones. Either can deliver a hard pinch, so make sure to reach for one with your net instead of your hand!

green crab

The green crab, *Carcinus maenas*, is closely related to the blue crab, but its hind legs are adapted for walking, not swimming. Look for green crabs in sea walls, tide pools, mud banks, and under rocks. Green crabs never get very big; the carapace of a large one may be only three inches wide. If you catch a green crab, turn it over to see what color it is underneath. Adult females have reddish-orange undersides; males are yellow or greenish underneath.

There are over 600 species of spider crabs in the world. The common spider crab, *Libinia emarginata*, has a carapace that may only reach a length of 4 inches, but its spindly legs may span a foot! Adult males have longer legs and pincers than females do. You can also tell males and females apart by the shape of their abdomens. Males have narrow, pointed abdomens and females have broad, oval ones.

Spider crabs are slow-moving and can be found crawling on all kinds of bottoms. Their shells are covered with short, hooked hairs, and often become overgrown with algae and small marine animals. Some species actually put bits of algae and debris in their hooked hairs.

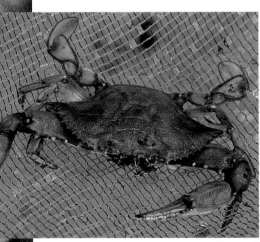

blue crab

spider crab

True crabs and anomurans

Blue, green, and spider crabs all belong to a large group called the **brachyurans**, or true crabs. All true crabs have flat, broad bodies and abdomens that fold tightly against the thorax. They also have three pairs of small jointed appendages that work together as mouthparts. Look for these just in front of the first pair of legs. In addition to the true crabs, there is another group of crabs called the **anomurans**. Anomuran crabs have only four well-developed pairs of walking legs; the fifth pair are small and upturned. The abdomen may be extended rather than folded under the thorax. Hermit crabs are anomurans, as are coconut and porcelain crabs.

Another anomuran is the mole crab. Mole crabs live on sandy shores near the water's edge. Constantly exposed to pounding surf, mole crabs alternately tunnel down into the sand, are unearthed by the waves, and tunnel down again. This is where they get their name. It's also where they get their food: mole crabs feed on the algae and other food particles that they strain out of the sand and water with their feathery antennae. To find a mole crab, dig in the wet sand at the water's edge. Males are about half the size of females, and spend about half the year clinging to the females almost like parasites.

Mole crabs can usually be found at the water's edge anywhere on the Atlantic or Pacific coasts. Just dig down a few inches.

Taxonomy

CLASS: *Crustacea*
ORDER: *Decapoda*

Brachyurans
FAMILY: *Portunidae (swimming crabs)*
SPECIES: *Callinectes sapidus (blue crab)*
Carcinus maenas (green crab)
FAMILY: *Cancridae*
SPECIES: *Cancer irroratus (rock crab)*
FAMILY: *Majidae (spider and toad crabs)*
SPECIES: *Libinia emarginata (common spider crab)*

Anomurans
FAMILY: *Hippidae (mole crabs)*
SPECIES: *Emerita talpoida (Atlantic mole crab)*
Emerita analoga (Pacific mole crab)
FAMILY: *Paguridea (hermit crabs)*

37

IN A SALT MARSH

Salt marshes are grassy coastal wetlands with creeks cutting through them. Some form where rivers meet the sea, others develop along bays or behind barrier beaches. A salt marsh changes over the course of a day. At high tide, most of the marsh may be flooded. As the tide goes out, it drains creeks and exposes mud flats. Although the water level, salinity, and temperature are constantly shifting, coastal marshes are rich in plant and animal life.

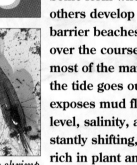

Grass shrimp

Things to bring

A salt marsh is a great place to look for arthropods. The following equipment will help you to catch them and will help keep you comfortable:
- old sneakers or water shoes, to protect your feet
- a small net or plastic container for scooping arthropods out of the water
- a plastic bucket to hold animals while you observe them.
- a hat or sunscreen to protect you from the sun

Arthropods you might find:

FIDDLERS

Look for fiddler crabs near tidal creeks and other low-lying parts of the marsh. Male crabs have one small front claw and one very large one, while females have two small claws. Fiddler crabs dig burrows that can be up to a foot long. When the tide gets high, they go into their burrows and plug the entrances with sand or mud. At low tide they come out again. Fiddlers feed on tiny bacteria and other organic matter. They get this food by sifting sand with their mouthparts. They filter out the edible particles and "spit" out pellets of indigestible sand. You'll often find these pellets piled up at the entrance to a fiddler's burrow. Larger pellets are evidence that a crab has been digging. When it digs, a fiddler rolls up little balls of sand and carries them to the surface with its legs.

SHRIMP

Shrimp have long abdomens that end in a telson, like a lobster. Their abdomens often bend sharply downward in the middle, giving them a zigzag shape. Many species of shrimp live far out to sea, but some can be found in coastal marshes. Along the east coast, look for shore shrimp and grass shrimp. You might scoop one up in your net or spot one clinging to underwater plants. Shore

shrimp are nearly transparent, and grass shrimp are greenish or reddish-brown. They are easy to overlook because their coloring camouflages them.

Shore shrimp

Hermit crabs depend on finding the abandoned shells of other animals, which they climb into and drag around with them. Without a borrowed shell, the hermit's soft abdomen is exposed and open to attack.

HERMITS

In fiddlers, green crabs, and other "true crabs," the abdomen is tightly folded against the thorax and protected by a hard exoskeleton. Hermit crabs, however, have long, soft abdomens. You won't often see the hermit's abdomen, though, because it's usually hidden inside a sea shell that the hermit is "borrowing." Tiny hooks on the hermit's abdomen grip the inside of the shell, and the hermit drags it around wherever it goes. Hermit crabs outgrow their shells from time to time, just like other arthropods, and must search for roomier ones. You might see a hermit investigating various possibilities by sticking its head and claws into empty shells. When it finds a promising one, it quickly slips inside. The crab may crawl off with the new shell, or hop back into its old one. Sometimes several hermits will even fight over a shell. Look for them in tidal creeks when the water is low.

Arthropods that might find you

Don't be surprised if some of the arthropods that live in the marsh find you before you find them!

Mosquitoes and green flies are among the insects that inhabit marshes, and during the breeding season females need a protein-rich meal of blood in order to produce their eggs. During their biting season, insect repellent may make your marsh visit more comfortable.

Taxonomy

PHYLUM: *Arthropoda*
CLASS: *Crustacea*
ORDER: *Decapoda*
  (8,500 species of shrimp, lobsters, crayfish and crabs)
FAMILY: *Ocypododae*
  (fiddler and ghost crabs)
GENUS: *Uca (fiddler crabs)*
SPECIES: *Uca pugilator (sand fiddler), U. pugnax (mud fiddler), U. minax (brackish water fiddler), U. crenulata (California fiddler).*
FAMILY: *Paguridae (hermit crabs)*
GENUS: *Pagurus*
SPECIES: *Pagurus longicarpus (long-clawed hermit) and P. pollicaris (flat-clawed hermit) are common east coast species. P. granosimanus (grainy hermit), P. samuelis (blue-clawed crab) and P. hirsuitusculus are common on the west coast.*
FAMILY: *Palaemonidae*
GENUS: *Palaemonetes (shore shrimps)*
SPECIES: *Palaemonetes vulgaris (common shore shrimps)*

You can clearly see that this fiddler crab is a male from its enlarged right claw, which is almost as big as the fiddler himself!

Horseshoe Crabs

Limulus polyphemus, the Atlantic horseshoe crab, can be found along the east coast of the United States. Other species of horseshoe crabs live in China, Japan, and the East Indies. All belong to the class *Merostomata*, a group of arthropods that contains mostly extinct species known only from **fossils**. In the winter, Atlantic horseshoe crabs stay offshore, partly buried in bottom sediments. In May, start looking for them along beaches and in tidal creeks. Horseshoe crabs spend the summer near shore, then head back to deep water when the days get short.

*Here is a horseshoe crab on its back. The two **Y**-shaped chelicerae are between the sets of legs and just behind the pointed part of the shell.*

Not quite crabs

Scientists believe that *Limulus* is more closely related to spiders and their relatives than to the other animals called crabs. This is because horseshoe crabs and spiders have some important physical features in common that they don't share with crabs. One feature is a special pair of feeding structures called **chelicerae** in front of their mouths. On *Limulus*, you can see the **Y**-shaped chelicerae on the animal's underside, right near the triangular point on the base of its shell. In spiders, the chelicerae are on the head and end in poison fangs. Crabs, such as blue crabs and hermits, don't have chelicerae. Instead they have mouthparts called **mandibles** that move from side to side.

Chewing legs and book gills

Horseshoe crabs eat marine snails, clams, worms, and other bottom-dwelling animals.

They eat as they walk, "chewing," or grinding up food with the bristly bases of their walking legs. The motion of their legs also moves the food forward towards the mouth, which is at the base of the chelicerae.

A horseshoe crab's hindmost legs look different from the other four pairs. They end in four petal-shaped projections instead of pincers. When a horseshoe crab walks, it raises its body with the first four pairs of legs, then pushes itself forward with the last pair. The hind legs are also used to move sand and mud out of the way when the crab burrows.

Horseshoe crabs use five pairs of **book gills** to get oxygen out of the water. If you look behind the crab's legs, you'll see the **operculum**, or covering, of each gill. Beneath each operculum are the many page-like folds of the gill. When a crab flaps its gills, fresh sea water moves across these folds and they absorb oxygen.

Here you can see one of the horseshoe crab's book gills and the many page-like folds inside it.

The bristly bases of a horseshoe crab's legs are used to grind up food.

Taxonomy

CLASS: *Merostomata*
(horseshoe crabs and
extinct related species)
ORDER: *Xiphosura*
FAMILY: *Limulidae*
SPECIES: *Limulus
polyphemus*

Life cycle

When horseshoe crabs mate, the male grabs onto the shell of the female and they crawl together up to the water's edge. The specially shaped claws on the male's first pair of walking legs help him hold on. The female scratches a depression in the sand and lays up to several thousand eggs in it. The male releases his sperm onto the eggs as they are deposited; then the pair moves on and repeats the process.

Horseshoe crabs mate from May through early July. They mate at high tide during a **spring tide**, when the water reaches farther up the shore than it will at any other time of the month. When the tide goes out, the crabs go with it, but their eggs stay behind on the beach. In the weeks that follow, the tide will continue to ebb and flow, but the water will not rise as high on the shore, so the eggs can develop in the damp sand without being washed away by the waves. By the time the next

spring tide washes them out to sea two weeks later, they will have hatched.

Newly hatched horseshoe crabs look different from their parents. They have no tails and they swim upside-down in the water. Over the course of many molts, their tails and book gills develop, and eventually they start swimming shell-side-up.

Though a female horseshoe crab may lay many thousands of eggs each year, few eggs will survive long enough to become adults. Gulls and shorebirds feast on the eggs before they hatch, and fish and other animals devour hatchlings and small crabs. Large horseshoe crabs, however, have no predators. No one is sure just how long they can live.

Horseshoe crabs become sexually mature when they are about three years old. At that point, they are about as long as a pencil. You can tell them apart by looking at their first pair of claws. In males (on the left), the claws look rounded like boxing gloves, while in females (on the right), they are narrow pincers.

After it molts, a small horseshoe crab like this one will stay buried in the sand until its new exoskeleton hardens. This helps it avoid large fish and birds that might make a meal of a soft-shelled crab.

Salt Water Aquariums

 salt water aquarium can help you learn more about shrimp, crabs, and other marine arthropods. You can often get a better view of their underwater activities through the sides of a fish tank than you can when you peer through the waves, and it's easier to keep track of individuals in a limited space. Of course, animals may behave differently in your tank than they would in their natural habitat. Combine your indoor observations with frequent trips to the shore to develop your understanding of arthropod behavior.

Starting out

Before you get any animals, make sure you have the time, space, and money to maintain an aquarium. Talk over your plans with someone who has experience with salt water tanks, or read up on them at the library. If you live along the coast you can collect local arthropods and sea water for your aquarium; if not, you will have the added expense of purchasing animals and chemicals for the water. If you do decide to set up an aquarium, gather the following equipment.

- A 10–30 gallon plastic or all-glass tank (metal seams can rust).
- A sturdy shelf, bench, or table to hold your tank.
- An air pump equipped with a filter. Under-gravel, box, and pump-circulating filters all work.
- Clean gravel or coarse sand. (If you are using an under-gravel filter, make sure to get gravel that is larger than the holes in your filter, otherwise the filter will clog.)
- Sea water, or a commercially prepared salt mixture to make artificial sea water.
- You may need to buy an aquarium heater if you want to keep tropical species, or a cooler if you want to keep cold-water animals in a warm building.

Setting up

1. Choose a spot for your tank away from heaters and out of direct sunlight. Once the tank is full, you will not be able to move it, so choose a permanent location.
2. Wash your tank with water (no soap) and set it on the bench or table where you plan to keep it. If you are using an under-gravel filter, position it now in the bottom of the tank.
3. Rinse your gravel or sand several times. To do this, put it in a bucket, cover it with water, then pour off the water.
4. Put a two-inch layer of the gravel or sand on the bottom of the tank.
5. If you are using a box or pump-circulating filter, set it up according to the manufacturer's directions. Connect any air hoses to the pump.
6. Cover the gravel or sand with sheets of paper so that it won't be stirred up when you add the sea water.
7. Fill your tank with sea water to within an inch of the top. After the tank is filled, remove the sheets of paper.
8. Turn on the pump to filter and **aerate** the water. Let the tank run this way for a couple of days before adding any animals, so that the environment you've created can stabilize.

Adding arthropods

Once your tank is working properly, you can collect or shop for arthropods to put in it. Add just a few at first; you might try a couple of shrimp, hermit crabs, and a small green crab. Help them adjust to the temperature of your tank by putting each in a small plastic bag with water from the place they were collected, and then floating the bags in your tank for half an hour. Then release the new animals into the tank, and keep an eye on them for a week. If they look healthy, you can add a few more. If any seem sick, release them where you found them or contact the supplier you bought them from. Although it is always tempting to add more animals to your tank, remember that overcrowding will lead to foul water and unhealthy animals.

Hermit crabs, barnacles, and shrimp do well in salt water tanks. So do small horseshoe crabs and small green, blue, and rock crabs. If you want to add animals other than arthropods, think about small fish, sea urchins, starfish, sea snails, mussels and clams.

Maintaining your aquarium

- Offer your animals a little food at a time, and remove any leftovers after an hour or so. Try feeding crabs once a week; they will usually eat small pieces of fish or squid. Barnacles and other animals that filter food particles from the water can eat fish food, brine shrimp or algae. Feed these animals every other day, and turn off the aquarium for an hour or two when you do. (Otherwise the filter, and not your animals, will get the food.)
- Add fresh water to replace any tank water that evaporates. Be careful not to add sea water! When water **evaporates**, the salts are left behind, and if you add new sea water, the tank will get saltier and saltier. If you want to use chlorinated tap water, let it sit overnight before putting it in the tank.

- Siphon off about a quarter of the water in the aquarium once a month and replace it with fresh sea water. This will keep the water clean enough for the plants and animals to stay healthy.
- If you have a box or outside filter, replace the glass wool when it becomes dirty.
- If algae grows on the inside of the tank, you can scrape it off with a glass microscope slide or a special tool you can get from a pet store or supply house. See page 62.

A note about fiddler crabs

Fiddler crabs need special housing. Give them a tank with shallow water and a good sized chunk of salt marsh peat to tunnel in. If you aerate the water, you can also keep a few small shrimp in the tank.

Down Under

Some arthropods spend part of their lives in the ground. With a little patience and a few simple tools, you can find out who lives under your back yard. You can also try looking for soil arthropods in a field, garden, vacant lot, schoolyard or the woods. Anyplace that you can get permission to dig in is a good place to start your search.

Things to bring
- a sturdy garden trowel
- a piece of light-colored fabric (an old sheet or pillowcase will do)
- a plastic bucket or several smaller containers
- a light-colored pan or tray
- optional: a hand lens, paper and pencil, and field guides to insects and other arthropods

Directions
1. Choose a place to dig. You might want to mark off a plot that is one foot wide by one foot long, and try to dig down to a depth of one foot.
2. Use your trowel to remove layer after layer of soil from the plot. Pile the soil on the piece of fabric, to keep it in one place.

In ½ square foot of soil we found—

What?	How many?
ant	||||| ||||| ||||| |||
isopod	|||
affad		
rolley	
live larv	
big ar	
bumbu	

3. If you notice any arthropods while you are digging, put them in your bucket.

4. Search through the soil you have piled up to see if it contains animals that you did not notice as you were digging. Save any that you find. Collect a few handfuls of soil in your bucket or a container, and put the rest back in the hole you have made.

What to do with your catch

Keep track of the different kinds of arthropods you unearth, and the number of each that you find. If you aren't sure just what to call a particular animal, sketch a picture to help you remember, or try using a field guide to identify it.

Bring your soil home and spread it out in a light-colored pan or tray. You may spot tiny animals moving around in the soil that you did not notice before, especially if you use a hand lens or a microscope to help you search. As you go through the soil, add any new discoveries to your list.

45

Woodlice

Woodlice, the sowbugs, pillbugs, and roly-poly bugs, are crustaceans. Unlike most of their crustacean relatives, however, woodlice live on land. Look for them in leaf litter, gardens, woodpiles, under logs and stones, and in other damp places.

What woodlice are like

Most woodlice are small, flat, and gray. Like other crustaceans, they have two pairs of antennae on their heads. The first pair is so tiny that you may not even notice it, but the second pair is easy to see. A woodlouse has seven body segments just behind its small head; these make up its thorax, or mid-section. Each segment has a pair of legs growing from it. The thorax is followed by the abdomen, which has six narrow segments. The last segment has two "tails," called **uropods**, growing from it. Pillbugs have short, inconspicuous uropods, but the ones on sowbugs are quite noticeable. Woodlice also have appendages called **pleopods** growing from the rest of their abdominal segments. Some of these are used as gills, to get oxygen from the air. Woodlice are scavengers—they eat decaying plants, fungi, and bits of organic material in the soil.

Family life

When woodlice mate, the male transfers sperm into the female's body with his second pair of pleopods. When the female is ready to lay her eggs, she deposits them in a special **brood pouch** on the underside of her thorax. She continues to carry her young in her brood pouch once they hatch, taking them wherever she goes. After about three weeks, the young are able to live on their own.

After a rain, or early in the morning when the air is still damp, you might spot a woodlouse crawling on a tree trunk.

Perhaps some woodlice have been nibbling on this mushroom.

A mother pillbug with her young.

Raising woodlice

You can keep woodlice in a terrarium. Add some well-decayed leaf litter, bark, or bits of moss to provide them with food. Keep the soil moist, but not damp or soggy. At times, you may want to take a few woodlice out and put them in a small dish or pan so that you can observe them more easily. Just remember that they need a humid environment in order to survive, and limit the amount of time you keep them out in the dry air.

Sowbug or pillbug?

When you first start looking at woodlice, they may all look the same to you. But if you study them closely, you can learn to tell different kinds apart. Two groups that you are likely to find are the sowbugs and the pillbugs. Sowbugs have flat, oval bodies and two distinct uropods. A pillbug's body, on the other hand, is more curved, or arched, on the top and its uropods are so short that you may not even notice them. When a pillbug is disturbed, it will roll up into a ball. A few species of sowbugs can do this as well, but most cannot.

Create different conditions within a small pan by arranging different kinds of soil, stones, and leaves inside. Add a few woodlice and watch to see where they go. Do they prefer to be on or under things? On soil, stones, or leaves? What will woodlice eat? Test out some different possibilities.

Taxonomy

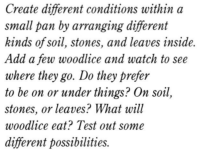

CLASS: ***Crustacea (crayfish, crabs, lobsters and relatives)***
ORDER: ***Isopoda (the isopods, which includes over 3,000 aquatic and terrestrial species) Armadillidiidae (the pillbugs) Oniscidae (sowbugs with three segments at the end of the antennae) Porcellionidae (sowbugs with two segments at the end of the antennae)***

47

Centipedes

In the woods, fallen leaves pile up on the ground. Together with broken branches, seeds, and dead animals, they form a spongy layer called **litter**. Leaf litter keeps soil moist by shielding it from drying sun and wind, and by gradually releasing soaked-up rain water. Litter is home to many small arthropods, including mites, woodlice, insects, and centipedes.

Centipedes

Most centipedes are nocturnal, but during the day you can find them in leaf litter and under stones and logs. They eat other arthropods, and will also prey on slugs, earthworms, and other animals. Some centipedes reach lengths of 5–10 inches and are capable of taking prey as large as toads and lizards. But most of the centipedes you find will probably be less than two inches long.

Each centipede has a pair of fang-like jaws with poison glands inside. When a centipede bites a prey animal, the poison stuns or kills it. This poison is rarely dangerous to people, but since the bite from even a small centipede can sting, take care when you handle them. You can pick up small centipedes with a pair of forceps or a plastic spoon. You'll need forceps for the larger ones.

The word centipede means "one hundred legs," but many centipedes don't actually have that many. Most species have only about fifteen or twenty pairs of legs. Centipedes have one pair of legs on each body segment. The last pair of legs is longer than the others, and some centipedes can use it to pinch. Some centipedes already have the number of body segments and legs characteristic of their species when they hatch. In other species, the young have fewer body segments and legs, and grow longer and leggier with each molt.

Some centipedes lack eyes and cannot see, but even those with eyes see poorly. It seems they are able to tell light from dark, but their eyes don't form pictures, the way ours do. Centipedes probably hunt by smell and by touch.

Centipedes like this common scutigera, Scutigera coleoptrata, *may escape the winter weather by coming indoors. If you find one around your house, treat it with care. Even a small centipede can deliver a stinging bite.*

Around the house

You are sure to find centipedes if you search under stones and through leaf litter, but you might also spot one in your bathtub! The common scutigera, *Scutigera coleoptrata,* lives in many parts of the United States and Europe. In the warmer parts of its range, it usually stays outside, but in northern climates it spends the cold weather in houses and other buildings. Sometimes a house centipede will slip into a sink or bathtub while it is hunting for insects. Unable to climb the slippery sides, it will stay trapped there unless a person rescues it. You might also see a common scutigera running across a floor or wall, or outdoors. Adults are one inch long, and their fifteen pairs of extra-long legs allow them to move quite quickly.

Taxonomy

CLASS:
Chilopoda (the centipedes)
ORDERS: *Scutigeromorpha (includes Scutigera coleoptrata, often found in houses) Lithobiomorpha (the stone centipedes; adults have 18 body segments and 15 pairs of legs; young have fewer legs) Geophilomorpha (the soil centipedes; 31–177 pairs of legs) Scolopendromorpha (21–23 pairs of legs)*

So far, over 2,500 species of centipedes are known world-wide.

49

ROBERT AND LINDA MITCHELL

Millipedes

illipedes, the "thousand leggers," avoid light, so look for them under bark, rotting logs, stones, and in leaf litter. Millipedes also live in caves, and some live in old earthworm burrows. A few kinds even live in ant nests, right alongside the ants!

Millipede habits

Most millipedes eat plants, particularly dead and decaying plants. A few kinds of millipedes are scavengers, or prey on small animals such as insects, worms, and centipedes. Millipedes, in turn, are eaten by larger animals such as toads and birds. Millipedes tend to be slow moving, but they do have ways of protecting themselves that may help them escape some predators. Most can coil their bodies into a spiral when they are disturbed, as pillbugs do, or secrete a strong-smelling liquid from "stink glands" along their bodies.

Millipedes hatch from eggs. Newly-hatched millipedes usually have just three pairs of legs and a small number of body rings. More rings are added with each molt. Some species are so small that even as adults, it would take ten of them lined up end to end to measure an inch long. Other kinds may grow to nearly a foot in length. Adult millipedes can have anywhere from 26 to more than 200 legs—more than you would want to count, but far short of one thousand.

How to tell a millipede from a centipede

Many people think millipedes and centipedes are pretty much the same, but scientists have decided that there are enough important differences between the two groups to place each in a separate order. If you find an arthropod with lots of legs, and you aren't quite sure what to call it, watch the way it walks and look closely at its legs. Millipedes seem to glide over the ground, as waves of motion pass along each row of legs. Centipedes wiggle more, as legs on opposite sides of the body take turns taking steps. Millipedes have two pairs of legs on each body "segment." (Scientists consider each segment of a millipede's body to be a double segment—two segments fused together—and often refer to it as a ring.) Centipedes have just one pair of legs per segment.

Scientists recognize over 10,000 species of millipedes, and there are probably many more.

Taxonomy

CLASS: ***Diplopoda
(the millipedes)***
ORDERS: ***Polydesmida
(eyeless millipedes with
20 body rings with flat-
looking backs)
Glomerida (short, wide
millipedes that look
like pillbugs)
Nine other orders***

Millipedes at home

You can keep a few millipedes in a
terrarium. Make sure you have
included some leaf litter or stones
for them to crawl under. Since millipedes prefer dark places, they can
be difficult to observe. You may
want to take them out from time to
time, and put them in a small container where you can watch them
more easily.

MILLIPEDES HAVE:	CENTIPEDES HAVE:
• a slow, gliding walk	• a fast, wiggly walk
• double body segments called rings	• single body segments
• two pairs of legs per body ring	• one pair of legs per segment
• rear legs that are the usual length, or shorter	• extra-long rear legs
	• poison jaws

The Berlese Funnel

A Berlese funnel can help you find the very small arthropods that live in soil and leaf litter. It will help you collect very tiny animals that you might otherwise overlook. You can make your own Berlese funnel from equipment you buy or find around the house, or you can order a funnel from one of the companies listed on page 62.

Materials
- a large plastic or metal funnel
- piece of coarse wire screen (a 1 centimeter or 1/4 inch mesh will do)
- wire cutters or tin snips
- a heavy glass jar *or* a three-legged stand to hold the funnel and a small glass vial
- fresh leaf litter or soil
- an adjustable desk lamp *or* a mothball and a board a little bigger than the large end of the funnel
- a jar lid or petri dish
- a hand lens or dissecting microscope

Directions
1. Cut a circular piece from the wire screen with the wire cutters or tin snips. Make the circle three or more inches in diameter.

2. Place the circular screen inside the funnel.

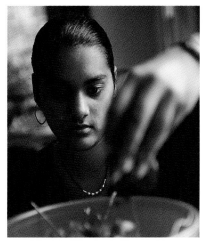

3. If you are using a purchased funnel that comes with a stand and glass collecting vial, slip the vial onto the small end of the funnel, and place the funnel in the stand. Otherwise, set the funnel in the glass jar.

4. Place several handfuls of soil or leaf litter on top of the screen. Make sure to use fresh litter that you've collected that day.

5. If you are using a lamp, turn it on, and position it so that the bulb shines down into the funnel. If you are using a mothball, tape it to the board, then cover the top of the funnel with the board. (Make sure the mothball is "inside," facing the litter.)

6. After about half an hour, lift the funnel and look into the collecting vial or jar. If you don't yet see any animals, put the funnel back in place, and give the light bulb or mothball more time to drive them out of the soil or litter.

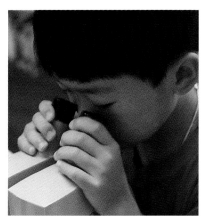

7. Put the animals you have collected in a jar lid or petri dish so you can take a close look at them with a hand lens or dissecting microscope.

8. When you are through, return the animals to the soil or litter, and take them back where you found them.

Arthropods you might find

Pseudoscorpions like this one are common in leaf litter and moss, under bark, and in houses. They have four pairs of legs and large pinchers. They eat mites and small insects, but are far too small to bite or pinch a person. They make up the arachnid order Pseudoscorpiones.

Mites are tiny arachnids that belong to the order Acari, as ticks do. There are tens of thousands of different kinds of mites in the world, and countless individuals. You may find dozens of them in a few handfuls of leaf litter! Some mites are parasites for part, or all, of their lives. Others are free-living predators who hunt for insect eggs and other miniature prey. Look for shiny, dark, beetle mites, and bright red velvet mites.

Safety Note: If you use a lamp, make sure the bulb is close enough to warm the litter, but not so close that it might melt a plastic funnel! If you use a mothball, set up your funnel outdoors, or in another well-ventilated area.

AT A POND

Ponds are shallow bodies of water with muddy bottoms. Because ponds are shallow, sunlight can reach even the deep parts, and aquatic plants can grow across most of the bottom. These plants provide food, shelter, and oxygen for a wide variety of freshwater arthropods.

damselfly nymph

54

Planning your pond trip
The equipment listed below can help you explore a pond. For your first pond trip, choose items that you already have on hand. After you have done some collecting, you may want to buy some of the other items that seem useful.

- Rubber boots, old sneakers, or water shoes to protect your feet.
- Bug repellent, to keep away mosquitoes and other insects.

- A plastic ladle or other small container, for scooping up samples of water and mud.
- A long-handled aquatic net, for collecting from deeper water.
- A light-colored pan, such as a dishpan or refrigerator tray, to hold animals while you observe them.
- A plastic bucket with a snug lid, for taking part of your catch home if you want to.
- A hand lens for magnifying tiny animals and getting a closer look at larger ones.
- An underwater viewer for looking at animals in the water. You can make a small one by taping plastic wrap over one end of a big tin can.
- A field guide to pond life, to help you identify unfamiliar arthropods.

Ways to look and things to look for
Grab a little bottom muck with a plastic container, ladle, or your fingers. Put the muck in a pan with some water and wait for it to settle. As the water clears, you may notice animals moving around that you didn't see at first.

Some spiders, like this Tetragnathid, build webs near water. They are able to catch mosquitoes and other flying insects as they emerge from a pond or fly above it.

Fishing spiders, like this one, can actually run across water. Special hairs on their legs help them stay on the surface. Fishing spiders can also dive down into the water to search for prey.

Check the leaves and stems of plants that grow in and around the water. Young damselflies, called nymphs, live under water and can often be found crawling on submerged plants.

Look closely at the sticks, stones and leaves you find in the water. Some will have arthropods clinging to them. Some may even turn out to be arthropods! Most caddisfly larvae make cases for themselves out of bits of vegetation, sticks, or sand grains. They feed on small animals, algae, and other organic matter that they scrape from rocks and plants. Caddisflies leave the water when they become adults.

Sweep a long-handled net through the water or use it to collect debris from the bottom. Perhaps a tiny crayfish will be among the arthropods you capture.

A safety note

A pond may be shallow compared with a lake or the ocean, but the water may still be well over your head. To be safe, do your collecting near the shore. Plan your pond trips with an adult, and always bring along a friend or two.

Taxonomy

CLASS: *Insecta*
ORDER: *Odonata*
  (damselflies and dragonflies)
  Trichoptera (caddisflies)
  Diptera (flies, mosquitoes, and relatives)
CLASS: *Arachnida*
ORDER: *Aranea (spiders)*
FAMILIES AND GENERA: *Pisauridae:*
  Dolmedes (fishing spiders);
  Tetragnathidae (spiders that
  build angle and orb webs);
  Tetragnatha (long-jawed orb weavers)
CLASS: *Crustacea*
ORDER: *Decapoda*
FAMILY: *Astacidae (crayfish)*

Aquatic Insects at Home

Most of the aquatic insects that you will find at a pond can be brought indoors for closer study. When you are through, return them to the same pond you collected them from. There, they will be able to find food, and the temperature and chemistry of the water will suit them. If you are unable to travel back to the same pond, then preserve the insects in alcohol and add them to your collection. That way, you will not release them in areas where they might cause problems, or fail to thrive.

Short-term housing

You can keep pond insects in an old refrigerator tray or a clean dish pan. Make sure to include a few aquatic plants and some pond muck for the insects to crawl on. If you only keep your specimens a few days, you won't have to worry about supplying food. Some of the animals you collected will hunt for others to eat, and others will feed on fresh or decaying vegetation. A plastic spoon can help you transfer animals from the collecting bucket to your tray or dish. You can also use it to scoop up individual insects that you want to take a closer look at.

Long-term housing

If you decide to set up a fresh water aquarium for pond animals, gather the following materials:

- A glass or plastic fish tank, 1 to 30 gallons in size.
- A sturdy bench to hold the tank.

- An aerator.
- Clean gravel.
- Some pond muck. If you wish, you can also add a chunk of soil, with plants rooted in it, from the pond's edge.
- Fresh pond water.

With a light-colored tray and a plastic spoon, you can get a better and closer look at your catch.

Directions

- Rinse your aquarium out with water, then place it where you plan to keep it. Make sure to choose a spot that is out of direct sunlight.
- Layer the gravel in the bottom of the tank and spread a little muck over it. If you have collected a chunk of soil, put it in a corner of the tank.

- Decide how deep you want the water to be in your tank, then add pond water to that level.
- Set up your aerator according to the manufacturer's directions, and make sure it is working properly.
- Collect and add insects.

Care and feeding

If you are keeping a variety of insects, you will need different kinds of food for them. **Predators**, such as water scorpions and dragonfly nymphs, will eat any smaller animals they catch. To keep from ending up with an empty tank, you'll need to limit the number of predators you keep, and continually add prey animals such as mosquito larvae, worms, and small crustaceans. Insects that eat plants or decaying organic matter will feed on the vegetation and pond muck in your aquarium.

Over time, as water evaporates from your tank, the water level will drop. Replace it regularly with freshly collected pond water.

This is a water strider, a prey animal for water scorpions and dragonfly nymphs.

Water scorpions

A water scorpion will creep slowly around on the submerged vegetation in your tank. Its long "tail" is actually a two-part breathing tube, which it sticks out of the water when it needs more air. Water scorpions have strong front legs, which may remind you of antennae, because they are often held out in front. They use these legs to grab their prey and draw it close to their beak-like mouths. Like other insects in the order *Heteroptera*, water scorpions have piercing, sucking mouthparts. They can deliver a painful bite if you pick them up by hand, so be sure to use a spoon to handle them. They also have wings, and sometimes fly at night, so cover your tank if you keep water scorpions.

57

Tiny Pond Dwellers

ome of the arthropods that live in ponds are so small you can barely see them. With the naked eye, they look like moving specks. With the right kind of microscope, however, you can see their miniature bodies, jointed legs, and antennae.

The compound microscope

You can use a **compound microscope** to observe any animal that is small enough to fit on a glass microscope slide and thin enough for light to pass through. Compound microscopes can magnify a specimen hundreds (sometimes even thousands) of times, making it possible to see things as small as individual cells. If you don't own a microscope and want to buy one, you can contact the supply houses listed on page 62 for models and prices. Student models start at about $35. More sophisticated and powerful microscopes are expensive, but you can sometimes buy an affordable used one from a high school or college that is upgrading its equipment. Also, check your own school to see if there are microscopes you can use.

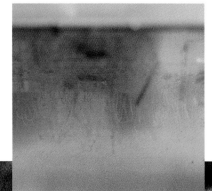

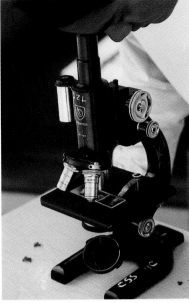

This compound microscope can reveal tiny animals that live in a single drop of pond water. The specimen goes on a glass slide.

Collecting tiny arthropods

Although it is difficult to see tiny arthropods, it is quite easy to collect them. Simply scoop up some pond water in a jar, or tow a fine-mesh **plankton net** through the water to get a more concentrated sample. You can also gather a little algae or duckweed from the surface of the pond, scoop up a bit of bottom muck, or scrape the slimy coating off a rock or aquatic plant. Most of the time you'll end up gathering animals along with the water, weeds, or slime. If you don't live near a pond, or when winter weather makes collecting difficult, you can order microscopic pond animals from a supply company.

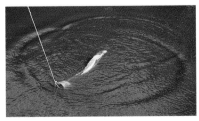

You can use a plankton net like this one to collect tiny plants and animals.

Observing your samples

When you get home, prepare your samples for observation. Scrape muck or slime samples into a light-colored pan and pour a little water over it. Float aquatic plants in pans of water as well. Allow jars of pond water to settle; leave the lids askew to allow fresh air inside. Once the samples have settled, look closely at them. If you notice any "specks" that seem to be moving by themselves, pick them up with an eye dropper and place them on a glass **microscope slide**. Or, simply put a drop of slime or pond water directly on a slide. Gently drop a **cover slip** onto the slide and look at it under the microscope.

Pond dwellers you might find

You may see tiny crustaceans called copepods swimming in hops, or spurts, through a sample of pond water. Copepods, like other crustaceans, have two pairs of antennae. Some species can rotate the longer pair to send a current of water streaming past their mouthparts, which filter tiny particles of food from the water. Other species seize food and bite it. Female copepods deposit their eggs into one or two long ovisacs. The females then carry their **ovisacs** around with them until

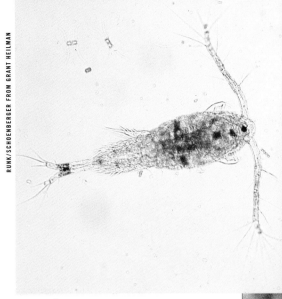

copepod

the eggs hatch. Some copepods are **parasites** that attach themselves to other animals, but you are more likely to find **free-living** species.

The *Cladocera*, or water fleas, are also crustaceans. Some species use their long antennae to swim, while others use them to hold on to objects. Many cladocerans have a shell or carapace covering their bodies. A few species are predators, but most filter algae, bacteria, and other particles of food from the water. They keep a current of water streaming past their mouths by moving their legs inside their shells. Water fleas can have very complicated life cycles. Often, only females will be present in a pond. These females reproduce without mating, and all of their young are also females. At other times, the females in a pond will produce male young. When these males mature, they will mate with females.

Other places to look

Tiny arthropods are all around us. They live in the sea, in soil, and in the scum that forms on a flower stem in a vase of water. Some even live on human skin! A microscope can help you find out more about the "invisible" animals that surround you.

Crayfish

Crayfish are common in rivers, lakes, ponds and streams. Some species climb around on land at night, returning to burrows in damp soil when they are through foraging for food. Many kinds of crayfish are easy to raise and interesting to watch. Collect some from a local pond or order a few live ones from a supply company (see page 62).

Housing

Keep crayfish in an aquarium or a plastic tub with a layer of clean gravel on the bottom. Some species do best in very shallow water that doesn't quite cover their bodies. Others need deeper water and a filter and aerator for their tank. If you collect your own crayfish, pay careful attention to the water level where you find them and try to duplicate it at home. Mail-order crayfish will arrive with care instructions. Most crayfish do best in clean, well-oxygenated water, so change the water daily if you are not filtering it. Tap water is usually fine for crayfish.

Put a few rocks in the tank so that your crayfish can climb out of the water from time to time. Rock piles or clean clay flower pots will provide burrows for them to hide in. If the tank is large with several hiding places, you can try keeping several crayfish in it. But keep an eye out for fighting and other aggressive behavior; these are signs that you need a bigger tank or fewer crayfish.

Feeding

Crayfish are scavengers and will eat all sorts of food. You can offer them bits of raw fish, meat, dog or cat food, and aquatic plants. Put the food right in front of them and if they don't start eating it within five minutes or so, remove it and try again later. Feed your crayfish three times a week, and change the water after each feeding. If you want, you can move each one to a small pan or dish for feeding so that it's easier to keep the tank water clean.

Here are two different kinds of tanks you can set up for crayfish. The shallow one (above) is better for species that live in shallow water and like to come out on rocks occasionally. The tank on the right is deeper, and has an aerator. If you don't use an aerator, make sure to change the tank water every day.

Observe your crayfish while you feed them, and make note of what they like to eat.

Crayfish anatomy

Pick up a crayfish and get familiar with the way it looks. You'll notice that it has a hard shell, or **carapace**, covering its fused head and thorax. On the head, look for:

- two large compound eyes on movable stalks
- two pairs of antennae. Both pairs are important sensory organs. The first pair, called the antennules, are shorter than the second, and contain organs that help the crayfish keep its balance.
- five pairs of jointed appendages that serve as mouthparts. One pair is also used to clean the antennae, and another moves water across the gills, which are underneath the carapace.

On the thorax, look for five pairs of walking legs. The first pair end in large claws which the crayfish uses to crush its food and to defend itself. Some of the crayfish you find might not have all ten of their legs. If a crayfish's leg is grabbed by a predator, or in a fight with another crayfish, it often breaks off. A tiny new leg will appear after the next molt and grow larger as time goes by.

Crayfish have swimmerets on the underside of their abdomens. In adult males, as in adult male lobsters, the first pair look different from the rest. These two swimmerets are long and hard and are used to transfer sperm to the female. Female crayfish tend to have wider abdomens than males, and smaller front claws.

Behavior

Watch how your crayfish use the various parts of their bodies and how they interact with each other. If you have a few crayfish and want to make sure you can tell them apart, give each one a distinctive mark with nail polish. Dry off the carapace with a paper towel so that the nail polish will stick. Over time, try to find out:

Notice the five pairs of walking legs and the swimmerets behind.

Taxonomy

*CLASS: **Crustacea***
*ORDER: **Decapoda***
*FAMILIES: **Astacidae,
Cambarinae**
(500 species worldwide)
Procambarus blandingi,
the species in most of
these photos, is common
in pools and slow
moving streams.*

Mark your crayfish so you can study their individual behavior.

- Whether your crayfish are able to swim.
- When your crayfish are most active. Observe them at different times of the day and night, on cloudy and sunny days, and with the room lights on and off.
- What a crayfish does when you approach it, or when another crayfish comes near.
- Whether particular crayfish "hang out" in specific parts of the tank.
- If the crayfish in your tank seem to get along as equals, or if one **dominates** the others by displaying aggressive behavior until they retreat.

61

Continuing

As you continue to study arthropods, you'll make new discoveries and raise new questions. Answers can come from people in your community, research and educational organizations, and library books. When deciding who to call on, remember that the phylum Arthropoda is a large and diverse group of animals, and that many people just study one particular group of arthropods.

People and places to contact

Ask if any teachers at your school are interested in insects, spiders, or marine arthropods. If there is a college or research center near you, find out if anyone on staff can meet with you or answer your questions by phone. Museums, aquariums, and nature centers often have educators who teach classes or will answer visitors' questions. Call ahead to make sure such a person will be available while you are there.

Check the yellow pages in your phone book for listings of local exterminators. These people usually know a great deal about pest insects. Your community may also have a county agent who is up-to-date on local arthropods that affect livestock, crops, and gardens. A local garden club or wildflower society can help you locate native plants to include in a butterfly garden.

Many organizations promote research on and conservation of arthropods. The Xerxes Society (10 SW Ash Street, Portland, OR 97204), for example, seeks to preserve rare invertebrates, including butterflies and other arthropods. Many of these organizations send their members magazines and research publications. Your local nature center, or a biology teacher or librarian, can help you find the organizations that would be most interesting for you.

How to Order Equipment and Supplies

The most enjoyable way to study arthropods is to collect as many different kinds as you can yourself. As for equipment, you'll be surprised at how easy it is to adapt everyday pans, bowls and other kitchen and hobby supplies to fit your needs. However, depending on the season or where you live, it can be difficult to find all the specimens mentioned in this book. Almost all of the equipment and many of the arthropods mentioned in this book can be ordered through the mail or by phone from a company called Carolina Biological Supply. If you want to order by phone, you'll need an adult with a credit card to make the call.

IN THE EASTERN US
Carolina Biological Supply
2700 York Road
Burlington, NC 27215
Toll free 1-800-334-5551

IN THE WESTERN US
Carolina Biological Supply
Box 187
Gladstone, OR 97027
Toll free 1-800-547-1733

Please remember: If you order live specimens, make sure you have everything you need to house and feed them before they arrive. If the specimens are not native to your part of the country, it is very important that you not release them into the wild after studying them—letting them loose in a new environment could disturb the ecological balance in your area. If you're not sure about whether a specimen is native to your area or not, ask the people at Carolina Biological Supply, or a biology teacher at your school. If you do have to kill a specimen, freezing it is the safest and least painful method.

If you can't find Crickets in or around your house (pages 10–11), you can order 12 live House Crickets for about $5 (cat. #L715) or a "Little Chirper" Cricket Cage, which comes with six live crickets, food, and a booklet, for about $12 (cat. #L717). If you want to try raising praying mantids (pages 20–21) but can't find any egg cases, you can order a set of three for $11 (cat. #L738). Another arthropod you may want to raise is a butterfly (pages 24–25); if you have

trouble finding a chrysalis, you can order a complete kit for raising Painted Lady butterflies (not the same as Monarchs) for about $20 (cat. #L915). Butterfly nets (pages 28–29) can be made, but you can also order one for about $8 (cat. #65-1346). For starting your own insect collection (pages 32–33) quite a few supplies can be ordered: Styrofoam mounting boards (cat. #65-4190) cost about $19 for a batch of 10; mounting pins come in packages of 100 in assorted sizes for about $7.50 each (remember to ask for sizes 0, 1, 2 and 3, cat. #s 65-4302–05); and small glass vials come in sets of 12 for about $5.00 (cat. #71-5212). You should be able to find woodlice (pages 46–47) in any patch of soil, but if not, you can order a dozen for about $6 (cat. #L624). Centipedes (pages 48–49) and millipedes (pages 50–51) can be ordered in groups of 3 for about $12 (cat. #s L642 and L645). It's easy to make a Berlese funnel, but you can also order a kit for $13.50 (cat. #65-4148). Large microscopes (pages 58–59) can be very expensive, but Carolina Biological Supply sells a Folding Pocket Magnifier for field trips (the 5X model, cat. #60-2110, costs $4.50; the 10X model, #60-2112, costs $7.50). For a more powerful home microscope, they also sell the Panasonic Light Scope, a 30X microscope with a light and batteries, for about $35 (cat. #59-4900). Fresh pond water with microscopic life (page 59) costs $3.50 per gallon (cat. #16-3380). And you can order three small Crayfish (pages 60–61) for $5.00 (cat. #L593).

ATTENTION TEACHERS: *Most of the equipment and specimens listed here are available at quantity discounts for classroom use. In addition to Carolina Biological Supply, these supplies are also available from Delta Education, Inc. (1-800-442-5440), ETA (1-800-445-5985), Science Kit and Boreal Laboratories (1-800-828-7777), Tweber and Companions (1-800-301-7592) and Wards Natural Science Establishment (1-800-962-2660).*

Glossary

aerate: to put oxygen into water, usually with a pump.

anomurans: a group of crabs that includes hermit and mole crabs.

ballooning: a way that spiders move around, by using strands of web silk as parachutes to carry them in air currents.

body ring: a section of a millipede's body, made up of two fused body segments and carrying two pairs of legs.

book gills: the breathing organs of horseshoe crabs. Book gills get oxygen from the water by opening and closing somewhat as books do, which allows water to pass over the many page-like folds of the gill.

book lungs: the breathing organs of some arachnids. Like book gills, book lungs extract oxygen by opening and closing like books.

brood pouch: a special place on the underside of a female woodlouse, where she deposits her eggs and carries her newly hatched young.

carapace: a protective shell.

cephalothorax: the joined head and thorax of spiders and other arachnids.

chelicerae (pl.): the special mouth-parts that horseshoe crabs, spiders, and some other arthropods have.

chelipeds: the claws of a lobster or other member of the order Decapoda.

class: a group of living things. Each phylum is divided into classes, and each class is further divided into orders.

classify: to organize living things into different groups.

compound eye: an eye made up of many simple eyes that function together.

compound microscope: a microscope that uses several lenses together to magnify images hundreds of times.

cover slip: the glass cover placed on top of a microscope slide to protect the specimen and the objective lens.

cultivated: grown and cared for by people. Cultivated plants and animals are often bred for particular traits, such as size or appearance.

Diptera: the insect order that includes flies, mosquitoes, gnats, and their relatives.

evaporate: to change state from a liquid to a gas.

evolve: for a species, to change form and characteristics over long periods of time.

exoskeleton: a hard outside body covering that protects internal organs, serves as a place for muscles to attach to, and prevents drying out on dry land.

fossils: the bodies of ancient plants and animals which have become mineralized.

frass: the waste products of caterpillars and other insect larvae.

free-living: not a parasite; able to live outside of the bodies of other plants or animals.

fruiting bodies: the parts of a fungus that produce spores which then grow into new fungi.

fungicides: chemicals used to kill unwanted fungi.

fused: joined together without seams.

genus (pl. genera): a group of related species.

gone to seed: A plant has "gone to seed" for the season when it no longer has any flowers and has released its seeds.

honeydew: a sweet liquid secreted by aphids and thornhoppers, and sometimes eaten by ants.

insecticides: chemicals used to kill unwanted insects, especially those insects that eat food crops.

introduced species: a plant or animal brought by people to a place outside its natural environment.

late blight: a disease harmful to potato plants, caused by a fungus.

litter: the top layer of the soil in wooded areas, made up of decomposing plant and animal matter.

mandible: the small mouthparts that crabs and other arthropods use to chew their food.

microscope slide: a thin piece of glass used for looking at specimens under a microscope.

molting: the process of shedding an old exoskeleton.

native species: a plant or animal which has evolved in the environment where it is found.

nectar: a sweet, nutritious fluid secreted by many plants to attract pollinating insects, such as butterflies.

nymph: the young of any insect with gradual metamorphosis.

63

operculum: the covering of a horseshoe crab's book gill.

order: a group of related families.

ovisac: a long pouch that female copepods deposit their fertilized eggs in.

parasite: an organism that lives in or on other organisms. Parasites typically weaken, and sometimes kill, their hosts.

peat moss: a dried moss available at gardening stores that can help new plants grow.

phylum (pl. phyla): a group of related classes, and the primary divisions in the animal kingdom.

plankton net: a net of very fine mesh for scooping plankton up out of the water.

pleopods: the appendages on the body segments of woodlice. The male uses his second pair of pleopods to transfer his sperm to a mating female.

pollinate: to transfer pollen from one flower to another.

proboscis: a long, straw-like mouthpart.

pupate: in complete metamorphosis, to pass through the stage between immature and adult body forms.

range: the geographic area where a species can be found.

regenerate: to grow back. Many arthropods can regenerate lost limbs.

resistance: the ability to withstand exposure to disease or harmful chemicals, such as insecticides.

scavenger: an organism that eats dead plants and animals, or garbage.

simple eyes: eyes capable only of detecting light and darkness.

species: distinct kinds of organisms.

spring tide: the time at which the tide rises the highest, which occurs twice a month.

swimmerets: small, paddle-like appendages that grow from the underside of a lobster's tail and help it swim forward.

taxonomy: a system of classifying living creatures, such as arthropods, by grouping them according to shared, uniquely evolved physical characteristics.

telson: the final part of a lobster's tail, also called the tail fan.

territorial: having to do with a given territory or area. A territorial arthropod may try to keep intruders away from a particular place.

thorax: the middle body section of an arthropod.

tidal creeks: creeks that run into the open sea. When the tide rises, sea water flows upstream into tidal creeks, and changes the environment for animals and plants living there.

tubercules: the bumps that line a lobster's shorter, "crushing" claw.

uropods: the appendages on the last body segment of woodlice.